D0088519

GOOD THINGS
COME IN
SMALL GROUPS

THE DYNAMICS
OF GOOD GROUP LIFE

Written by a small group
consisting of

Steve Barker
Judy Johnson
Rob Malone
Ron Nicholas (coordinator)
Doug Whallon

INTERVARSITY PRESS
DOWNERS GROVE, ILLINOIS 60515

InterVarsity Press is the book-publishing division of Inter-Varsity Christian Fellowship, a student movement active on campus at hundreds of universities, colleges and schools of nursing. For information about local and regional activities, write IVCF, 233 Langdon St., Madison, WI 53703.

Distributed in Canada through InterVarsity Press, 860 Denison St., Unit 3, Markham, Ontario L3R 4H1, Canada.

Charts on pages 144-46 are adapted and reprinted from A Church Council Guidebook by permission of Parish Life Press.

Quotations from Scripture, unless otherwise noted, are taken from the Revised Standard Version of the Bible, copyrighted 1946, 1952, © 1971, 1973, and used by permission. Those marked NIV are from the Holy Bible: New International Version. Copyright © 1973, 1978, International Bible Society. Used by permission of Zondervan Bible Publishers.

Cover photograph: David Singer

ISBN 0-87784-917-X

Printed in the United States of America

Library of Congress Cataloging in Publication Data
Main entry under title:

Good things come in small groups.

   Bibliography: p.
   Includes index.
    1. Church group work—Addresses, essays, lectures.
2. Small groups—Addresses, essays, lectures.
I. Barker, Steve.

| BV652.2.G56 | 1985 | 259'.7 | 85-778 |

ISBN 0-87784-917-X

17	16	15	14	13	12	11	10	9	8	7	6	5
99	98	97	96	95	94	93	92	91	90	89		

Preface

God is constantly renewing his church. While the world keeps changing, God's arsenal of spiritual resources remains constant. Prayer, faith, Scripture, love and worship are pillars of renewal. Throughout the ages God keeps drawing his people together so that they can experience his presence, receive his gifts, reach out to others and reaffirm their commitments. As the writer of Hebrews states, "Let us consider how to stir up one another to love and good works, not neglecting to meet together, as is the habit of some, but encouraging one another, and all the more as you see the Day drawing near" (Heb 10:24-25).

This book comes out of our individual and corporate commitment to the local church. In recent years the church has been rediscovering one of God's timeless building blocks of spiritual vitality—small groups. With the rising tide of interest in small groups, we lobby for standards of excellence. Such groups can be dynamic expressions of the grace and power of Jesus Christ in the lives of people. By "people" we don't mean those few who think they have achieved spirituality. We mean all who recognize their fragility, brokenness and sin but who are seeking to grow into the likeness of Christ.

This book also reflects our experiences as a small group. Each person is a combination of hurts and hopes. Each of us has experienced the grace of Christ in our life. Together we have grown by the power of Jesus Christ funneled through a dynamic small group. We have encouraged one another and have benefited from the breadth of our perspectives and personalities.

In addition, all of us have been involved in small groups in our home churches and in training small group leaders for various churches. Each has served on Inter-Varsity Christian Fellowship staff at least ten years, serving from New England to California.

Ron Nicholas, our small group leader, is a member of Colonial Congregational Church of Edina, Minnesota. Steve Barker is the associate pastor for evangelism, adult education and church administration at First Presbyterian Church in Yakima, Washington. Rob Malone belongs to Beverly Heights United Presbyterian Church of Pittsburgh, Pennsylvania. Judy Johnson lives in Minneapolis, Minnesota, and is a member of Normandale Lutheran Church. Doug Whallon teaches in the adult Sunday-school program at Grace Chapel, Lexington, Massachusetts.

Our understanding of groups is rooted firmly in Scripture, as the whole tenor of this book will attest. Since the leadership of such groups is pivotal, we have devoted several chapters in part one to unlocking key concepts on how to lead effectively. A block of four chapters (part two) examines the central ingredients of balanced small group life. Part three develops a strategy for integrating small groups into the total mission of the church. The last section, part four, provides a practical compilation of specific ideas, strategies and helps.

May God grant *you* the joy of participating in a dynamic group dedicated to our Lord Jesus Christ.

Part 1
Basics of Small Groups

Chapter 1
We Need Each Other

Becky backed out of her driveway. On the seat beside her was her Bible and a piece of paper with a few scribbled directions on how to get to the Wrights' house. She was on her way to a small fellowship meeting that a friend at church had invited her to.

Arriving at her destination, Becky parked her car and sat for a few moments. Thoughts whirled through her mind. What would this group be like? She was looking for some friends. Having lost her husband several years before, she needed emotional support. She also wanted to grow in her knowledge of the Bible. She slid the key out of the ignition, gathered her things and walked to the front door of the Wrights' home.

Norma Wright, a friendly and robust woman, opened the door and greeted Becky warmly. Several others had already arrived and were enjoying a piece of pie and casual conversation in the living room. Introductions were made. Maynard, Norma's husband, invited Becky into the dining room where the refreshments were being served. Other members of the group arrived, and after a few minutes the meeting began.

Marilyn sat down at the piano, and the group sang several hymns and thanked God for this opportunity to be together. Notes were sometimes missed, and someone was singing off-key. Becky chuckled to herself. It felt good to worship God with people who wanted to honor and acknowledge his presence—even with sour notes!

After a brief time of worship the group leader asked everyone to form pairs to respond to several questions:

"On a piece of paper write down three things. First, what kind of weather describes your mood this evening? Second, is there some way that Christ has made a difference in your life this week that you want to share with your partner? And finally, what do you think it means to be a growing disciple of Jesus Christ?"

After a few moments of silence and writing, the room exploded with conversation as members shared their responses with one another. Becky found the questions interesting and was grateful for the chance to tell someone what she was thinking.

The third question introduced the topic of the Bible study that evening—what it means to be a growing disciple. Becky learned two things as they studied John 15. First, a disciple of Jesus Christ is one who is seeking to abide or live in Christ, to depend on him every day. Becky knew she needed to rely on Christ more fully. Second, a disciple is one who produces fruit. Becky was not sure what it meant to "produce fruit," but she felt that by sticking with this group she might find out. The meeting concluded with members praying for each other's concerns and needs.

Becky was glad she had come. The warmth and love she felt encouraged her. Their attitude toward God and the Scriptures was something she wanted. Their care for one another led her to believe that this group of people knew they needed each other.

We do need each other. God intended it that way. He made us to be in relationship with him and with each other. Much of our growth is dependent on the quality of such relationships. These can often be best built within the context of small groups of committed Christians.

Belonging

As we pass through life we belong to various small groups. Each of us was born into a small group, a family. Here we began to discover who we are and to have our most basic needs met. All of us have a need to belong. Our security is often rooted in knowing that at least one other person loves and cares for us. We need to know and be known by others, to love and be loved.

As we grow, our circle of interpersonal relationships widens, and we begin to include others beyond our immediate family. We join scouting, Little League and other peer groups. High school and college offer sororities, fraternities, athletic teams, drama groups and ski clubs. And as adults we may be members of churches, school boards, bridge clubs, camping clubs, bowling leagues, professional groups. Each of them ties people together to meet needs or to work on a common task.

Within the church, people also gather in all kinds of groups. Many of us are part of more than one. *Groups in the church are people joined together to meet needs and/or to do the ministry of the church,* each group focusing on a particular aspect of that ministry. There are Sunday-school classes, church boards, church committees, Bible study and prayer groups, choirs, men's groups, women's groups, youth groups, outreach groups, support groups. The purposes of the groups vary, and we join the ones that fit with our gifts and goals. But most of us choose to be in one or more of them also because we hope that some of our most basic needs will be met: our need to know and be known, to love and be loved.

Church groups must meet these needs to some extent, as well as fulfill their stated purpose, or they are not likely to succeed.

The choir, for example, whose purpose is to praise the Lord in song, may be composed of excellent voices. But if the members constantly squabble about solos or the tempo or which hymns to sing, the group will fail to do what it set out to do. Such a choir will not honor God no matter how good the voices sound. A session or church board that is run efficiently but whose members do not know one another will not likely model Christian leadership as God would want them to; their service in the church will be ineffective. The apostle Paul reminds us in 1 Corinthians 13 that love is the hallmark of the Christian person or group. A group of young people who are growing in respect and love for each other as they study the Scriptures together and "ham it up" on the volleyball court is probably doing the ministry of the church more than the choir whose members don't get along. The youth group will grow because its members are cared for and nurtured.

Why Small Groups?
Spiritual growth, like emotional growth, does not occur in a vacuum. It comes as we relate to others in the body of Christ, his church. Why then have so many Christians failed to find spiritual stimulation in their local church? One key reason is that churches today, in general, lack the essential community that characterized churches for centuries. The people you sat next to in church last Sunday very likely do not live in your neighborhood. And even if they do, chances are that they will move away in three years. These are facts of life. We just don't get to know, *really know,* the people who are our brothers and sisters in Christ if we meet only in a large group that draws from a twenty-mile radius and that changes constantly. By meeting in smaller units we make intimacy at least possible.

One of the best ways to learn and apply the Scriptures to our life is to study them with a small group. In a small group we can encourage and help one another discover and obey God's Word in ways that are simply impossible when the whole church meets together. God gives gifts and experiences to each of us that will contribute to the growth and maturing of others, but only if we meet in groups small enough and with people committed enough to each other to share. A group like Becky's can be a significant force in the lives of those involved. It can also provide a base from which the members can reach out and minister to others beyond the group. Members may help each other witness to non-Christian neighbors and friends and together see them come to a personal relationship with Jesus Christ—often resulting in new members coming into the group.

Small groups are an integral part of just about any church's life. As the parts relate to one another in an atmosphere of love and security, submitting to Christ's leadership and to one another, the results can be powerful: the church grows and upbuilds itself in love. A network of all kinds of small groups within the church, doing various ministries, enables the church to grow and make a difference in the world.

Small *koinonia* (Greek for "fellowship") groups meeting in homes can be the church's basic building blocks for personal discipleship, as we will see in chapter twelve. Becky's group began as a nurture group, that is, people meeting together to encourage each other's growth in Christ. As new people joined the group, however, it changed to meet new challenges, needs and opportunities. Several in the group were new Christians, and they were helped in their growth by the group as a whole and by several members one to one. The group is currently preparing to lead a Bible for Today weekend of discipleship training for other new Christians. The opportunities for small groups within the church are virtually limitless.

Most groups begin with a flourish of high expectations and good intentions. But unfortunately not all groups succeed. Why? Because sin disrupts the harmony that God intends us to have in our interpersonal relations. We may not feel comfortable or secure with that other person in the group. Or perhaps the group began well but is beginning to drift or get sluggish. Maybe it has lost its sense of direction as well as its momentum.

What makes a small group work effectively, so that everyone can experience it as a source of both comfort and stimulation? In the chapters that follow we will look at the ingredients for creative, dynamic small groups and suggest ways to keep groups functioning. Good groups do not happen automatically. They take time, commitment, understanding and the power of the Holy Spirit. But God has used and continues to use small groups in the lives of his people and in the work of his church. They are worth the effort.

Chapter 2

I Am the Church, You Are the Church

God makes the church, we don't. Just as we did not decide who would be a member in our family and who would not, so it is with the church. We can choose not to use our gifts, or we can pull out of some committee, but once we are God's children we are in the church and that's that.

We are the body of Christ. There really is no such thing as lone-ranger Christianity. Paul Tournier makes this point when he says there are two things we cannot do alone: one is be married and the other is be a Christian.

The real truth about the church is that we are *a chosen people.* We have not chosen God or each other so much as he has chosen us. Peter explains it in his letter to the church at Rome: "You are a chosen race, a royal priesthood, a holy nation, God's own people, that you may declare the wonderful deeds of him who called you out of darkness into his marvelous light. Once you were no people but now you are God's people; once you had not received mercy but now you have received mercy" (1 Pet 2:9-10).

Peter wants us to remember where we have come from—nowhere! Once we were "no people." Oh, we tried to be a community; but it was based on beauty, intelligence, a choosing of one another based on personality, your meeting my needs, a choosing of one another *because of* . . .

The good news is that now we have received mercy. God has chosen us just as he chose people in the past. Our potential as a community is not based on our work but on God's. And our forgiveness in Christ is the cornerstone on which we build. He chose a kingdom of priests so that the world might know of his wonderful deeds.

God's choosing us and our experience of this community are, however, often quite distinct experiences. We may agree intellectually and theologically that we are God's people, but how do we experience this truth in our churches? One thing is clear: both the Scriptures and our lives tell us that we don't experience the fullness of Christian community in large group worship or at church banquets. We do find it in small groups. If the church is serious about fellowship, it must break down into smaller units.

Small Groups in Scripture

Jesus poured his life into twelve disciples, expecting that they would change the world. That was some small group. Imagine Matthew, a tax collector detested by Jews, with Simon the Zealot, sworn to hate all that Rome stood for. Or Peter, headstrong and bold, dining with James and John, while they jockey for positions of power. This group went through some tough times!

Yet Jesus chose these twelve and promised that their love for one another would make an impact, causing others to believe in him (Jn 17:21-26). In Acts Jesus turns his work over to them; they were to declare his kingdom in Jerusalem, Judea, Samaria and "to the end of the earth" (Acts 1:8). God chose his people that the whole world might be blessed.

Paul tells us in Philippians what will happen in the world when people observe Christian unity: they will be drawn in. But often, rather than going into the world, the church stays put. We expect others to come to us and visit our buildings to experience the love of God. We need to design a strategy for penetrating the world so that our community can be seen by the world and make an impact on it.

True Friendship

Dan Hendricks came to Harvard University looking for what he called true friendship. His parents were atheistic psychiatrists, but as a child he had read the Narnia Chronicles by C. S. Lewis and had developed from them an entire world view, his ideal of true friendship. At Harvard, as he met with a small group of Christians, for the first time in his life he came to know people who lived by his standard of friendship. He saw the gospel lived out in a group of believers that were experiencing the fellowship of the Spirit, Christian community. About eight weeks later, after studying the Gospel of Mark, Dan became a Christian.

The world is hungry for the community the church can offer, and it will look for it elsewhere if the church fails to provide it. Several years ago my father died. As I returned home to be with my mother, I found myself with several people who had been regular customers at the tavern my father owned for eight years. They too had come to honor my father and comfort my mother. I was struck with the kind of friendship they had developed which Christians so often fail to have.

My experience at church has at times left me disappointed. I know of others who came because they needed community, but who did not find it in the regular worship service. Every church must deal with this problem if it is to demonstrate that Christian

community is better than what the world has to offer. True friendship can happen in the church, but it takes small groups.

Christian fellowship is having every member of your small group
call you when your mother dies or you lose a baby during preg-
nancy. It's being able to share about failures in parenting and
marriage, being cared for when the job becomes too much for you,
being encouraged in developing gifts of leadership and hospitality.

Greg and Marsha, a young Christian couple, were both committed to Christ, but the Word of God had become for them more and
more just words, less and less an experience of God. A young
associate pastor of their church invited them to be a part of a small
group. It changed their lives. They developed relationships with
other Christians who held them accountable in their personal
growth with God and with whom they could share personal problems. When Greg and Marsha moved to California they began another small group, and when they moved to Boston they began yet
another. For them, Christian community as lived out in a small
group became a must for Christian living.

Advantages of a Small Group

In his book *The Problem of Wineskins* Howard Snyder points to
a number of advantages of a small group within the church.

It is flexible. The group can change its procedure readily and
meet the needs of its members. My own group changes every three
months.

It is mobile. You can meet in a home or even an office. It is not
bound by a building. Think of the three thousand people in Acts 2
meeting in homes!

It is inclusive. You are missed if you don't come. The small group
is open to all types of people.

It is personal. The small group creates a place where my needs
and the needs of those others who commit themselves to it can be
met. I remember our small group studying Psalm 46 after my son's

bike was stolen right out from under him. What a great help it was for Julie and me to have around us friends who could not only affirm with us the truth of the psalm, that God is our refuge and our strength, but who could also *be* Christ's body to us in a personal way through their listening and praying.

It is risky. A small group puts us at the edge of adventure in our Christian life. As we discover ourselves and others through conflict, care and confrontation, we grow. God works in our lives through the others.

It is an excellent way to evangelize. The true friendship of a small group will be noticed by the world, if the church is actually in the world.

It is not easy to begin a small group strategy in the church. For some it is too much of a change. But I've seen it work. In my church in California a small group of about twelve became convinced that what was happening in their group was important enough to share with others in the church. So each member learned how to lead another small group. They risked themselves and changed our church. Now almost half of the congregation is involved in small groups. This was particularly helpful when for over a year the church was without a pastor. It grew even without professional leadership.

God is calling us to a great task as a church. The church is not a holy place, but it is a holy people called by God to declare his mighty deeds to the world. Annie Dillard says that "we are itsy bitsy people living itsy bitsy lives raising tomatoes when we could be raising Lazarus" *(Pilgrim at Tinker Creek).* The practical nature of small groups can be key in penetrating our world. They can help us raise Lazarus.

Chapter 3

The Four Ingredients of Good Group Life

How do you bake a good small group? We have all been in groups which were half-done, too dry or too sweet. What recipe for small group life will blend together the essential ingredients in just the right proportion?

The life of the early church as reported in Acts 2:42-47 gives us a good idea of the special characteristics of Christian groups needed to bake a good small group.

They devoted themselves to the apostles' teaching and to the fellowship, to the breaking of bread and to prayer. Everyone was filled with awe, and many wonders and miraculous signs were done by the apostles. All the believers were together and had everything in common. Selling their possessions and goods, they gave to anyone as he had need. Every day they continued to meet together in the temple courts. They broke bread in their homes and ate together with glad and sincere hearts, praising

God and enjoying the favor of all the people. And the Lord added
to their number daily those who were being saved. (NIV)
These believers were devoted to four ingredients essential for vibrant Christian life: nurture, worship, community and mission.

Nurture
First, they were devoted to the apostles' teaching (2:42)—what we
now hold as part of the New Testament. Through their devotion
to the inspired words they received the spiritual food needed for
healthy Christian growth, growth into the likeness of Christ (Eph
4:13).

Nurture, as we will see more fully in chapter eight, involves
growth in both mind and spirit (Rom 12:2). God can nurture us
from Christian literature, films, tapes, lectures, sharing and many
other sources. But for most small groups nurture comes directly
from studying the Bible using the inductive Bible study method
(see pp. 140-41). All Christians need the empowering words of God
flowing into them if they are to maintain spiritual vitality and grow
in their fruitfulness.

Think about the groups in your church. Do any lack the energy
to accomplish their ministry because they are spiritually stagnated,
malnourished? Have some of the church boards lost their zeal for
their mission? Are Sunday-school classes diminishing? Do the mission circles occupy their time with gossip and coffee cake? Do the
prayer groups fumble in futile attempts to pray effectively? Perhaps
they need to analyze their spiritual diet and schedule in some
regular feasting from God's Word.

Worship
As Christians continually take God's Word into their lives, their
knowledge and love for God increases and worship springs forth.
Worship, which we will discuss more fully in chapter nine, is the
second essential ingredient for Christian group life. It flows from

our growing knowledge of God into praising and honoring him. It is adoring him for who he is and expressing that love to him. Acts 2:43 reports, "Everyone was filled with awe" (NIV). *Awe* is amazement, respect, reverence or wonder. Believers worshiped "with glad and sincere hearts, praising God." Our thankful spirits should break into singing out of joy for what God has done for us!

On a recent trip from Texas to Minnesota, my four-year-old daughter, Jenny, said, "Daddy, let's sing songs that will make God happy." That's the clearest definition of worship I've heard. Genuine worship brings joy to God! Is there a sense of awe, amazement and excitement about God in your group? Do you ever break into singing spontaneously because you can't hold back the joy of the Spirit?

A group which has experienced fifteen minutes of genuine worship together cannot move easily into petty arguments about church business. Worship unites like nothing else. If your small group is dull, disunified or disintegrating, encourage true worship as part of the agenda. Even a church board might benefit from a few moments of praising and adoring God. Try it next time before jumping into a hard issue and see how the rest of the meeting goes.

Community
Devotion to inspired teaching and response to God in worship are closely related to the fellowship we enjoy in Christian community. Community is the third essential ingredient for Christian groups. The church in Jerusalem was devoted to fellowship, or *koinonia*, as it is called in Acts 2. "All the believers were together and had everything in common. Selling their possessions and goods, they gave to anyone as he had need" (vv. 44-45 NIV).

Christian community is not merely a subjective feeling of belonging. It's different from membership in a bowling league, tennis club or civic group. Christian community, as we will see further in chapter ten, is more akin to the commitment of love and obligation we have toward members of our own families. It is devotion to one another based on the experience we share of God at work saving us from the "corrupt generation" around us (Acts 2:40 NIV) and knitting us into effective teams of change agents in the world. The outcome of life in community is that we are knit together in love and built up as whole people (Eph 4:12-16). This happens as we share needs, confess sins and faults, bear each other's burdens, encourage each other, listen with care and intercede in prayer.

The reality of our oneness in Christ is often expressed in practical ways. When my car failed to start once in ten-below-zero winter weather, Steve and Cathy (a couple in our koinonia group at church) loaned me their brand new car so that I could drive to work. When my wife, Jill, returned from the hospital with our new twin girls, we enjoyed several meals brought in by members of the same small group. We cried together when one member told of a car accident and problems at work. We all feel the pain when a couple's child is in the hospital. We celebrate together when God answers our prayers.

Is close Christian caring evident in your group? Are members united and committed to each other—so much so that they would sacrifice their material possessions to help a member in need as did the church in Acts?

Unity in Christian community does not mean people always agree on issues. Rather, we agree on recognizing our mutual experience of God's grace. But a Christian group does not exist solely for its own gratification and support. In Christ's community we are not to be cliquish. We have a mission beyond our members.

Mission

Mission is the fourth ingredient of vibrant group life. Christian groups exist to reach out and share the good news of Christ's love to people in need. We are the body of Christ, his avenue for extending his love and power to transform individuals and society. As we touch those around us, the Spirit puts them in touch with God and helps them grow into the likeness of Jesus. The flow of God's grace through us may first make an impact on the people closest to our group, but its power can extend to the ends of the earth.

The concept of mission includes such things as evangelism and social action. It also includes what is often called world missions, but it is broader than that. The concept covers everything from telling a neighbor about the Lord, to bringing a meal to the sick, to sending a couple of members of the group to Africa to learn how the church here can assist the church there.

Mission often starts with encouraging and praying for the individual ministry of each member. Our group prays for Lynn as she lives out her Christian faith among faculty and nursing students where she works. We listen and give her encouragement as she shares about a friend facing a crisis. We pray, and she later reports how God has worked.

At times, however, the entire group cooperates in outreach. In December our group (with help from friends and family) bought Christmas gifts for a couple dozen residents of a treatment center for mentally retarded adults. The year before, these people had not received any presents or special visits at Christmas, as they had no family or friends to care for them. But God cares for them, and we took the opportunity to show some of God's love.

The early believers demonstrated the love and power of God to the world around them: "Many wonders and miraculous signs were done by the apostles. . . . [They enjoyed] the favor of all the people. . . . The Lord added to their number daily those who were being saved" (Acts 2:43-47 NIV). Does your church have a clear mission statement (see example, p. 124) which members are aware of and committed to? Does each group or committee in the church understand how it fits into the overall mission? Are the groups advancing the outreach of members of the church or merely meeting to keep the program rolling?

Some groups need help to clarify the specific task God has for them. A good place to start might be to ask each member to write a brief statement which describes their group mission and how it fits into the overall mission of their church. The group can then discuss the different statements and work toward consensus.

Combining the Ingredients

Every group needs all four ingredients to some degree, but because of the diversity of gifts and the various tasks to be performed in the church, some groups will emphasize one particular ingredient, while other groups will emphasize others. (See figures 1-4.)

If you are a church leader, take a moment to list the various groups in the church and see where they focus. Does some area come up short? If so, what is its impact on your overall mission? What can be done to bring greater balance? Then look at each group to see if it is weak because one or more of the four ingredients are lacking. For example, are the Sunday-school classes poorly attended because no attention has been given to building community among members? Is the young married's group spiritually shallow because there is little or no biblical nurture? Does the board of elders lack spiritual vitality because worship somehow doesn't fit on the agenda? Is the charismatic fellowship group cliquish and self-centered because members are not involved in service beyond themselves?

Christian leadership often involves helping gifted people and specialized groups maintain a proper balance and stay on course. Once a problem is identified, church leaders may need to lovingly confront the leader of a specific group with its problem and then provide the appropriate training so that he or she can bring in the other elements of group life.

Koinonia Groups

Some small groups try to balance all four ingredients in their ac-

Figure 1. Groups with a special focus on *nurture*.
Sunday-school classes
Bible study groups
Book discussion groups
New member (new believer) classes
Confirmation classes

Figure 2. Groups with a special focus on *worship*.
Choirs and other musical groups
Prayer groups
Charismatic fellowships
Renewal groups

Figure 3. Groups with a special focus on *community*.
Support groups
Men's fellowships
Women's fellowships
Young couples' groups
Youth groups
Care groups

Figure 4. Groups with a special focus on *mission*.
Gospel teams
Evangelistic groups
Social-action committees
Missions committees
Visitation groups
Board of deacons
Board of elders
Renewal teams
Neighborhood Bible studies
Service groups

Figure 5. Koinonia groups with a balance of all four ingredients.

tivities (see figure 5). That, in fact, is the model we will focus on in the rest of the book. We will call this type of group a *koinonia group* since it combines the four ingredients of Christian group life we observed in the early fellowship of Acts 2:40-47.

Koinonia groups help members develop fully integrated Christian lives, which is essential if we are to "present every man mature in Christ" (Col 1:28). Our tendency, left on our own, is to follow hard after the facet of Christian living we like best, but Scripture and experience both point out the error of such imbalance. Burnout comes when Christians are overactive in mission without getting enough nurture. Dryness results if we get a lot of nurture and community without enough worship and mission. Small groups committed to *whole* Christian living help keep us all in balance. Christ is Lord of all areas of life, and balanced koinonia groups demonstrate that reality.

The four ingredients work together to strengthen a koinonia group, as Inter-Varsity Christian Fellowship has proved and modeled among college students. They need not all be given equal time in each meeting, but all should be included to a significant degree on a regular basis, *perhaps* every meeting. Figure 6 suggests some ways a group can bring about or enliven their nurture, worship, community and mission, both in their meetings and beyond. Often all four can be related to the main theme of Bible study. While

parts two and four of this book will give much greater detail on
how to enrich your group's life, figure 7 shows one group's six-
week plan, which relates each aspect to the Scripture being studied
that week.

Component:	Nurture	Worship	Community	Mission
Definition:	Being fed by God to grow like Christ.	Praising and magnifying God by focusing on his nature, action and words.	Fellowship centered around the experience we share as Christians.	Reaching out with the good news of Christ's love to people in need.
Goal:	Growth of the mind and spirit toward the image of Christ.	To bring joy to God.	To knit us together in love and build us as whole people.	To help people know God and become like Jesus.
Suggested activities:	☐ Discussing: the Bible inductively, books, lectures, tapes. ☐ Memorizing Scripture. ☐ Sharing with each other. ☐ Praying. ☐ Meditating.	☐ Praying. ☐ Singing. ☐ Reading worshipful passages from the Bible or other books. ☐ Writing and reading poetry. ☐ Writing a letter to God.	☐ Sharing with prayer partners. ☐ Bearing each other's burdens. ☐ Helping each other develop gifts. ☐ Eating together. ☐ Re-creating together. ☐ Going on a retreat or to a conference. ☐ Interceding for one another.	☐ Praying for non-Christian friends. ☐ Reading books on evangelism. ☐ Sharing the gospel with a specific group. ☐ Befriending an international student. ☐ Sharing care for a needy family or refugee. ☐ Raising money for world hunger relief. ☐ Praying for unreached peoples.

Figure 6. Ingredients of small group life.

Week	Nurture	Worship	Community	Mission
1	Study Acts 2:42-47. Explain the four components.	After explaining worship, pray one-word prayers of praise (such as names for God).	Serve popcorn. Do "Warm Up" (pp. 164-65). Describe yourselves.	Pray for non-Christian friends. Invite new person to next group meeting.
2	Review the four components. Have a Bible study in *Discovering the Gospel of Mark,* chapter one.	Sing a worshipful hymn. In prayer, focus on Christ's lordship.	Use "Who Am I?" (p. 164). Start prayer partnerships.	Discuss developing friendships with non-Christians and pray together.
3	Mark 2.	Have five minutes of silent meditation, focusing on the love of God.	Do "Journey of Faith" (p. 169).	Introduce a gospel outline. Pray. Plan a social event for your non-Christian friends. Pray about inviting people.
4	Mark 3.	Read a passage from *Knowing God.* Respond in prayer. Have each one write a prayer of praise and read as a prayer.	Continue with "Journey of Faith."	Introduce some pattern of prayer for world mission (p. 177).
5	Mark 4.	Read a worshipful psalm. Discuss briefly. Pray together.	Use "Color Me" (p. 171). Think of a color that would describe each person in the group.	Discuss the mission field of your small group.
6	Mark 5.	Have all share what you've learned about worship in the last five weeks.	Use "Weather Report" (p. 170). Plan a weekend small group retreat.	Formulate a covenant for your group (pp. 142-43).

Figure 7. Sample plan for the first six weeks.

One group, studying Acts 4, planned around the theme of boldness in evangelism. They got their nurture from the Bible study
itself. Community was strengthened when members shared their
fears about witnessing and discussed difficulties they had experienced; members encouraged each other. Their worship included
prayer that followed the pattern given in Acts 4:24-30. They prayed
for boldness in specific areas where members could share Christ—
with neighbors, on the job, with a friend, and so on—and thus
experienced mission together.

But it is not only Scripture that can be the unifying factor of
the four components. It can be prayer. Prayer is nurture when we
not only speak to God but also listen for his message to us. It can
help build community when members intercede for each other and
bring the needs of the group to God. It is worship when we praise
God. And it is mission when we intercede for people who need
God's love near us and around the world.

Communion also involves all four ingredients, and many small
groups have been deeply bonded as they celebrated communion
together. We are nurtured as we take part in the Lord's Supper. We
receive a special blessing when we partake of the cup and the
bread, which 1 Corinthians 10:16 calls the "cup of blessing." We
are also nurtured through the Scripture that is read and the teaching that often accompanies communion.

Communion is also a celebration of worship. Christ said, "Do
this in remembrance of me" (1 Cor 11:24). When we remember
God—who he is, what he has done—we worship him. The communion service includes prayers of thanks and hymns of worship
(Mt 26:30; 1 Cor 11:24).

Our Christian community life is both portrayed and strengthened
by the Lord's Supper. To eat the bread is, according to 1 Corinthians 10:16-17, to participate in the body of Christ. "Because there
is one bread, we who are many are one body, for we all partake of
the one bread" (v. 17). We are united as we experience God togeth-

er. "Participation" literally means we share something in common: the death of Christ for us. This is the basis for our new life with Christ in Christian community. Communion is the agape feast (dinner of love) for the Christian community.

Communion celebration is also an act of mission because in it "you *proclaim* the Lord's death until he comes" (1 Cor 11:26 NIV). In Matthew 26:28 Jesus says, "This is my blood of the covenant, which is poured out *for many for the forgiveness of sins.*" As we drink the cup, we remember why he died and we are motivated to carry out our mission of announcing God's forgiveness.

Blending the Ingredients

Just as eggs, flour, sugar and spices are blended together to bake a good cake, so the four ingredients blend in the total makeup of group life. They do not work in isolation. Let's look at seven ways they interact.

1. Worship strengthens community by uniting our focus on God. Small group unity is the result of our oneness in Christ. God made us one when he baptized us by his Spirit into newness of life in Christ (Rom 6:1-5; 8:9-11). And as we experience God's work among us, we grow even closer to each other. Ephesians 1 opens praising God for his plan to unite all things in Christ. We share the common purpose of bringing praise to God's glory (Eph 1:12). As we take our eyes off each other and look together at the greatness of Christ, we are drawn together in his purpose—to *unite* all things!

When it comes to questions of what, where, when and why,
not all of us can see eye to eye.
But all of us can agree The Who
because Christ Jesus is living in you.

Just as families that pray together stay together, so groups that worship in unity will be bonded in community.

2. Close community enhances group worship. Or, to put it

another way, playing together helps us pray together.

Interpersonal skills need time and opportunity to develop. Team work requires knowledge of each other's gifts and a willingness to trust each other. This is as vital for group prayers as it is for group sports. I have seen this in both volleyball and Bible study. If members of a group have learned to let each other hit the ball on the volleyball court, they may also learn to let each other speak; they will listen to each other in a Bible study. Sensitivity to others is important in both activities. The free flow of interaction between members in the group is vital for fellowship in prayer and corporate worship. I have often noticed that when I come to a group for the first time, I don't feel free to worship at once. I first need to know some of the members better so I can feel at home. Recreational time with the group can be a big help here.

3. Worship is a response to nurture. As our minds and spirits receive God's Word, we grow in our appreciation of his greatness. Our best response to God's revelation of himself is to praise and adore him. We should not be content merely to know facts about God. Rather we should use our knowledge about him as a basis for meditating on his nature. The more we know about God from his Word, the more we love him and desire to worship. A small group nurture experience should result in a greater appreciation for who God is. If worship is not happening frequently it may be because we have settled for junk food when God has invited us to a banquet meal. "Taste and see that the LORD is good!" (Ps 34:8).

4. Worship leads to mission. As we worship God and deepen our relationship with him, we begin to share his view of the world. We learn to love people as he does. Furthermore, our excitement about God as King of the universe motivates us to share this joyous friendship with others. In Acts 4:24-31, the Christians worshiped God, the sovereign Lord, and afterward spoke the Word of God boldly.

One summer I was leading a small group at Bear Trap Ranch,

a training center for Inter-Varsity Christian Fellowship in Colorado. Our group went into Colorado Springs to share the gospel with people in a large park. We were having trouble starting conversations with people, so our group gathered under some trees to pray. We praised God as Lord of our time and Lord of the park where we were. We asked God to lead us to people whom he was already preparing to hear about him. Worshiping Christ as Lord helped us overcome our self-consciousness and fear. We gained a new perspective on witnessing. We began to see how God was already speaking to others. And he led us into several deep conversations with people eager to hear more about Christ.

5. Nurture energizes mission. Just as our physical bodies need food to continue to work, so a small group needs to feed on the words of God to have power for mission. If a small group tries to do evangelism or social action without the nurture of God's Word, the members become thin, undernourished. In time their mission activity is in jeopardy because the members become too spiritually weak to keep working.

While in seminary I was in a small group that decided to study the minor prophets (Amos, Hosea and others). As a result of what we learned about God's concern for the poor, our group decided to help an organization which gave assistance to poor people in the inner city of St. Paul. We went to a house owned by this organization and helped clean it from top to bottom. We also prayed regularly for one of our members who worked with migrant workers in the city. As we learned about the injustice to the poor which the book of Amos speaks against, we decided to write letters to our congressional representatives about the poor of our own nation.

6. Mission strengthens community. (It is also true that lack of mission weakens community.)

When Paul wrote to the Philippians, he called them partners in the gospel because they had gone through the same struggles with opposition as he had in presenting the gospel (Phil 1:5, 30). They were united in witness, "with one mind striving side by side for the faith of the gospel" (Phil 1:27). If a small group works together sharing the gospel, they grow closer to each other. They learn to work together and support each other as a team. Facing opposition, they learn to "stand firm in one spirit" (Phil 1:27). Several Christian groups at the University of Minnesota learned this lesson one year when they distributed thirty thousand copies of the New Testament and led students to Christ through dozens of small group Bible studies. Prior to this mission the various Christian groups had made several attempts to establish unity. It took working together in a common mission to knit them together in a unified Christian community. In a similar way churches from various denominations are brought closer together when they cooperate in a Billy Graham evangelistic crusade.

If a group never engages in mission, it loses its common purpose and starts to become disunified. If a small group is not serving others, it becomes self-serving, lazy, unhealthy. Consider the example of the church at Corinth. Because their focus was internal and not on their mission to the world, they were divided and self-centered about the use of their gifts (1 Cor 3, 12—14). But a small group active in mission will also grow in community.

7. A strong community can accomplish a great mission. As a sense of community develops, the group can give individuals the love and support they need for personal growth while they reach out to others.

As a group grows together, it develops a unified sense of the particular mission God has given them (such as sharing the gospel with new neighbors). The members also developed a set of expectations for group involvement. For example, each member may agree to learn the basic content of the gospel and start a friendship with a non-Christian.

Although most groups need several weeks of interaction before a consensus is reached, some groups are formed on the basis of a predetermined commitment. To join a certain small group, for example, each member agrees: (1) to have a daily Quiet Time, (2) to pray daily for a non-Christian friend, (3) to share the gospel with one friend each week, (4) to read *Out of the Saltshaker,*[1] and (5) to train another Christian in evangelism. Usually groups that start with a predetermined commitment need to reconfirm or revise their agreement after they have worked together for a few weeks and developed a greater sense of community.

One of the best ways to strengthen community and commitment in preparation for mission is for the group to formulate a group covenant. This is a statement of group consensus on purpose. The process of writing a covenant helps members clarify their desires and agree on how to help each other accomplish the group goals. It should provide objective criteria for evaluation and accountability. For example, the group can have each member write out a basic outline of the gospel and hold each person accountable for learning it. (See chapter six, pages 63-64, and chapter thirteen, pages 142-43, for more about covenants.)

To maintain the proper balance of nurture, worship, community and mission—the balance agreed on by the whole group—requires more than consensus and covenant, however. It requires leadership as well. We turn in our next chapter to look at this key element.

Chapter 4

Leadership—The Critical Factor

Without adequate leadership a small group is doomed. Some deficiencies and frustrations groups can compensate for and still have a healthy life together. But without wise, loving leadership a group will suffer from an inhibited beginning, stunted growth and accelerated demise. And who needs that?

Good leadership unlocks a small group's potential. A good music conductor guides the orchestra into producing harmony. A football quarterback coordinates the team with a specific play to score a touchdown. So the leader of a small group helps members clarify their purpose and reach it. With a good leader people will take off their masks and find the freedom to give and receive love. Spiritual nurture produces spiritual growth. Thanksgiving to God becomes irrepressible. We experience God's love and extend it, within the group and then beyond its boundaries.

The Need for Christian Leadership

Washington, Lincoln, Churchill, Gandhi—most of us respect the great leaders of the past. In the last twenty years, however, the reputation of political leadership in general has deteriorated. Instances of corruption, abuse of power, financial mismanagement and deceit have planted seeds of suspicion in a whole generation. We view today's political leaders with skepticism.

Has our wariness of leadership stifled the growth of leadership in the church? Perhaps. But for the most part the Christian community still respects its leaders. Why then are so few people willing to assume Christian leadership?

Biblical examples of eager and able leadership are inspiring. Isaiah responded to God's plea of "Whom shall I send?" with a resounding "Here I am! Send me." Daniel, Deborah and David, other Old Testament heroes, heeded the call as well. However, because leadership is so demanding and human beings so insecure, we often avoid God's call to leadership. Moses made God wait for him while he exhausted his repertoire of excuses and rationalizations. And God had to go to great lengths in Jonah's case to retrieve and redirect him toward the right mission field.

One of Jesus' primary purposes was to build spiritual leadership. From among his many disciples he selected twelve to invest in heavily. These twelve he trained to lead and guide the early church. But their response was not always unbridled enthusiasm. Peter waivered. James and John quarreled. Thomas doubted. Judas betrayed. The rest deserted. Finding Christian leadership isn't always easy.

Paul had a similar experience when he planted the gentile church in the Mediterranean basin. He labored long and hard to prepare Timothy for pastoral ministry. But despite the apostle's tutelage, Timothy's confidence began to dissolve. Paul had to remind him "to rekindle the gift of God" (2 Tim 1:6) and not to "neglect the gift you have" (1 Tim 4:14). As pressures mounted,

Timothy was naturally inclined to grow tired rather than to call on God's Spirit "of power and love and self-control" (2 Tim 1:7). Yet all indications are that Timothy maintained his ministry, growing in faith and faithfulness.

So where does that bring us? To a God of generosity. He withholds nothing we need. He has given us his very own Son and lavished his grace freely on us. Since God has given every believer spiritual gifts, we can be quite certain he has distributed plenty of leadership ability for the church's vast needs. God has given gifts of administrating, teaching, pastoring and serving. These gifts enable his people to take positions of leadership.

The question is, Are we willing to serve as leaders? Are we like Paul—establishing churches and strengthening Christians everywhere? Or are we like Timothy—willing to try but lacking confidence? If we are like Timothy, we are off to a good start. Paul's message of encouragement in 1 and 2 Timothy is for us today as much as it was for Timothy.

Many of us, however, don't have Timothy's open attitude. Several reasons may account for this.

"I'm unable to lead." Maybe we do find formal leadership uncomfortable, awkward, even painful. But note: "Each has received a gift," Peter says, which is to be employed for one another's benefit (1 Pet 4:10). We have gifts! What are yours? Serving, teaching, giving, providing hospitality? The important thing is that we use our abilities, talents and gifts as an act of obedience to our Lord and Savior so the body of Christ may be built up. (But beware! Many of the gifts mentioned sound like the activities that make for good small group leaders! I suspect, however, that you are reading this book because you sense that you may have some leadership potential. Pursue it!)

"I'm unwilling to lead." This attitude is more often felt than verbalized. The issue revolves not around leadership aptitude but spiritual obedience. The simple truth is that if God has given us

the ability to be effective leaders, then we must *use* those abilities. He gave them for the benefit of others. So if I am a leader but unwilling to serve as one, I have a problem; I need to do some major business with God.

"I'm not sure I can lead." This is often a function of inexperience or lack of training. Many people have the skills and gifts to develop into strong small group leaders. It simply requires a willingness to practice and learn. This book should help.

What the Small Group Leader Does
We have defined a small group as people joined together to meet needs and do the ministry of the church. The purpose of a small group leader, then, is to help that happen. It means assisting the group in joining together, meeting needs and doing ministry. Sounds simple. It's not.

First of all, the biblical way of leadership stands in stark contrast to the way the world operates. Leaders of past and present societies have led, for the most part, by political influence, military might, intimidation, power plays, financial leverage, charisma and glamour. They sought status, power, security and wealth. But God's leaders are radically different. Jesus taught and demonstrated what has been aptly called the upside-down kingdom. In this kingdom, servanthood replaces domination.

Even Jesus' disciples got confused as to which way was up. In Mark 10, James and John lapsed into the world's approach. They asked Jesus to give them positions of authority over the other ten disciples in the kingdom they expected Jesus to usher in. When the others realized that James and John had asked this of Jesus, they were indignant. Why? Probably because they wanted to make the same request but hadn't had the nerve! Jesus confronted them by underscoring the new leadership approach shown by his own personal ministry. His model was clear: "For the Son of man also came not to be served but to serve, and to give his life as a ransom for many" (v. 45). His teaching was also clear: "Whoever would be great among you must be your servant" (v. 43).

The biblical model of leadership is built on twin concepts: (1) a servant serves by leading, and (2) a leader leads by serving.

Jesus demonstrated the first principle, that *we serve by leading,* by taking the risk of calling people to follow him. By being a leader he exposed himself to being misunderstood, criticized, ridiculed and even murdered. While such potential costs make us uncomfortable, we know that the benefits possible from such risk taking more than compensate. Jesus' service allowed us to be forgiven and to have an ongoing right relationship with the eternal God. For us, willingness to lead may result in a small group that is truly effective in reaching its goals.

Someone in the small group has to serve by initiating and guiding. Especially in the early stages of the group's life, the leader plays a crucial role in helping the group establish a direction and gain momentum. The designated leader usually serves the small group by:

1. Providing sense of purpose and vision. The leader reminds the group of its purpose. He or she suggests possible commitments and concerns that will shape the identity and activity of the group.

2. Initiating activities. The leader helps members get to know one another, both during and outside group meetings.

3. Encouraging others. The leader involves group members in the life of the group, helping them to use their abilities and resources to serve the group through hosting, providing refreshments, singing, leading studies and so on.

4. Setting expectations. The leader models openness and interest in the group. He or she must be willing to take risks by resolving conflicts and clarifying commitments and intentions.

5. Organizing logistics. The leader helps arrange details of early meetings (time, place, location, necessary resources) and communicates them to all the members.

Every time I lead a new small group, several uncertainties creep into my mind. Am I being too directive or too low key? Am I being too aggressive or too passive? Am I too formal or too casual? Too structured or too spontaneous? Will the group respond to me? Will they see my love for Christ? Will they recognize my desire to help?

I've concluded that these anxieties and pressures are natural and normal. They are occupational hazards that come with leadership. And, for the most part, they decrease as the small group's identity increases. The important thing to remember is that in offering leadership we serve the Lord and his people.

The second biblical concept is that we *lead by serving*. Jesus, the servant of God, serving person after person, is the theme stamped on virtually every page of the four Gospels. Jesus served his followers. He not only washed their feet but also calmed them in their storms, taught them in their confusion and prayed for them in their weakness. He served the masses. Not only did he feed the thousands but he also healed the sick, cleansed the lepers, clothed the naked, guided the lost and forgave the penitent. Zacchaeus needed a new start, Nicodemus a new perspective, the woman at the well a new relationship. All were people with definite and real needs: each needing to be served, each being served by Jesus—servant par excellence. "I came that they may have life, and have it abundantly. I am the good shepherd. The good shepherd lays down his life for the sheep" (Jn 10:10-11).

Jesus, our model as servant, maintained several balances that often elude us. First, Jesus served God and people simultaneously. It was not an either/or proposition but both/and. His service to God compelled him to serve the lost. Second, Jesus remained both people-centered and task-oriented. Again, it was not one at the exclusion of the other. Jesus cared and responded sensitively to those around him. At the same time he knew his mission and never lost its message or its urgency. The basis of Christ's balance is clear. He knew that only when program and message intersected with people would he produce the desired result. People would find peace with God.

Launching a small group requires lots of service. When a group starts, someone must decide on the who, when, where, why and how. That translates into placing phone calls, reserving rooms, arranging chairs, making coffee, offering rides, reminding people and, finally, making introductions. Such nitty-gritty work is thankless but necessary. It's the behind-the-scenes effort that often determines whether the initial small group meeting is a miserable failure or a promising beginning. A Christian who is going to lead must perceive the needs and provide the service. So roll up your sleeves and get on with the task of serving. It's the only way of building the kingdom of God.

Qualities of a Small Group Leader
In the last few years I've seen some small groups led by people who had strong, natural leadership instincts but who were new Christians or immature in their faith. The small group would get off to a weak start and never jell. Or it would start with enthusiasm and fade like a shooting star. The basic problem was leaders who looked good but lacked the spiritual stamina and substance to build a group intent on growing in Christ. Paul advised Timothy to be careful in the selection of leaders. A leader "must not be a recent convert, or he may be puffed up with conceit and fall into the condemnation of the devil" (1 Tim 3:6). In selecting small group leaders or in evaluating your own readiness, it is therefore important to evaluate spiritual stability and maturity as well as gift and talent. Many of the New Testament epistles were written to new churches just getting organized. Frequently these letters list qualities that a person should have to be an elder or deacon: temperance, sensibility, hospitality, gentleness, to name a few (see, for example, 1 Tim 3; Tit 1; 1 Pet 5). Although no biblical passage describes qualities specifically for small group leaders, consider

which attributes would be desirable for such a position. While these qualities should describe all Christians, they are all the more relevant to anyone serving as a leader.

But the most important quality of a leader is a hunger and thirst for God. This will give direction to all the other skills. As Christians we must desire to "be conformed to the image of his Son" (Rom 8:29). The beatitudes should be our trademark. We are being "changed into his likeness from one degree of glory to another" when we allow the Spirit to reign in our lives (2 Cor 3:18). God promises that this process of Christian growth will occur in each of us unless we let sin dull our love for Christ.

Thus Paul pleads with the Ephesians, "I . . . beg you to lead a life worthy of the calling to which you have been called, with all lowliness and meekness, with patience, forbearing one another in love, eager to maintain the unity of the Spirit in the bond of peace" (Eph 4:1-4). So God promises to renovate our lives in Christ, provided we cooperate with his lordship. As we use the gifts of the Spirit, God produces in us the fruit of the Spirit (Gal 5:22). In short, God is rebuilding our character, our core personality. Gradually we shed our conformity to the world and are transformed to God's standards. This process is accomplished as we seek God by setting aside time to worship and praise him, to study and apply God's scriptural principles, and to reflect and pray. These personal disciplines honor God and increase our own depth, joy and fulfillment. Small group leaders must earnestly and consistently seek to grow in their own relationships with Christ. "With my whole heart I seek thee" (Ps 119:10).

While many qualities are useful, three are indispensable:

1. *Commitment to grow in our own relationship with Jesus Christ.* This is the source of growing in godliness.

2. *Commitment to get involved in other people's lives.* A small group leader needs to be interested in each person in the group. He or she needs to get to know them—by asking questions, by

attempting to communicate care and demonstrating spiritual concern. A leader who is only interested in the group's welfare and not the welfare of those comprising the group will seem condescending, cold, standoffish, self-righteous. Only the love of Jesus in us can generate such personal caring.

3. Commitment to influence others. None of us have it all together, but God has enabled us to help one another. Sometimes people cry for help in clear and unavoidable ways. All we need to do is listen and respond. But many people quietly guard their concerns and weaknesses. A sensitive small group leader discerns those needs and weaknesses and creates an environment for growth. The Bible is overflowing with words that reflect influence—*encourage, comfort, exhort, admonish* and *teach.* The quality we need is one that enables us to upbuild, feed and strengthen other Christians.

Those with healthy starts on these three commitments have the potential to lead and serve effectively. For they seek to develop a godly character; they love with the love of Christ; and they assist the group members in Christian growth.

If you already are a small group leader, don't let these last paragraphs overwhelm you. Instead, allow them to remind you of key priorities. I find that when I graph my Christian development, it is not simply a constantly rising line of steady progress. Rather it contains surges and lapses, progress and regress. I need to regularly evaluate how I'm doing and to keep going back to the basics. Often that means renewing my daily time with God in prayer and Bible study, making sure my spiritual compass is again pointing at Jesus. The world would love to press us into its mold so that we don't have time for or interest in God and others. We must resist that pressure, and choose rather God's priorities in our lives.

Skills of a Small Group Leader

Small group leaders are not born. They are developed. With work, we can acquire numerous skills. For instance, as we learn to ask better questions or seek more practical applications (see chapter eight), the quality of our group Bible studies will increase. As we gain a better understanding of the stages of development a small group undergoes (see chapter six), our ability to guide the group will become more sensitive. A number of strategic skills we can develop if we are willing to work on them. The list that follows is far from exhaustive, but good leaders will want to keep these in mind and practice them regularly.

Listening. I may need to bite my tongue if I speak too much or am overly eager to contribute. Restraint may give a reluctant member more ease in participating. "Be quick to hear, slow to speak" (Jas 1:19).

Asking questions. Many people want to be known but find it hard to clear initial hurdles. Ask nonthreatening questions that make people feel comfortable and draw them out. Ask about their background, interests, hobbies and friends. What do they like to do with leisure time, with holidays? In other words, learn to be an effective host or hostess.

Improving participating in your studies. Too often leaders dominate the time given for Bible study. A good discussion of a passage gets everyone involved in discovering the content, discerning the meaning and applying the principles to life. It can happen if the leader prepares sufficiently and designs good questions.

Familiarizing yourself with the stages of a small group. (Chapter six will provide a quick review.) If you can recognize where your group is in its stage of life, you can better guide it toward its own goals.

Communicating care, warmth and reassurance. It's hard to smile when we are feeling nervous, but our effort to convey warmth will pay rich dividends. We need to extend this caring when we make initial contacts—long before the first meeting. Whether I make an introductory visit or a phone call, the care communicated will make a great difference. As the early meetings begin, welcoming words, a warm smile, eye contact or a hearty handshake can help dissolve hidden tension and anxiety. *"Glad* to see you!" "How are *you?"* "Thanks for taking the time to come!" Think ahead about how you might welcome each one.

Reflecting openness within the small group. This is the opposite of being defensive. It's hard not to react negatively to criticism. It's especially tricky when the criticism is unwarranted, unrealistic or uninvited. Within limits, however, it is good to absorb such feedback in a nonreactionary way so members can see our interest in their opinion.

Involving the members in the ongoing life of the group. We can help a group develop cohesive unity in its early life by asking for volunteers to help with mechanical tasks. As time goes on, the group will want to determine its own goals and activities. The more consensus achieved, the stronger the solidarity of the group. This may sometimes mean we spend a lot of time talking together, but in the long run it proves well worth it. We should invite group discussion, partnership and initiation. Our goal in this is group ownership.

Helping solve problems. Perfection is divine; problems are human. You can expect occasional confusion, disagreement or tension. It's going to happen in any and every human relationship. In some cases, a problem reflects the need for more love or clearer communication or greater kindness. Other times a difficulty requires greater toleration or partial compromise or deeper understanding. Often it means that priorities need to be sorted, purposes refocused and commitments reaffirmed. Of course, occasionally the leader is the problem. More frequently, though, the leader will be in a position to identify a problem and facilitate its constructive resolution. He or she will help most by facilitating an atmosphere that is affirming of the people but sensible about conflict. Blessed are the peacemakers.

Being prepared for the meetings. To prepare for a gathering is more a discipline than a skill. Experience sharpens our ability. We must pray for people's openness and God's activity. We need to digest the text so that we can shape relevant questions. We need to know how we'll use the limited time of the meeting to make the most of it. There is no short cut to thoughtful preparation.

Developing and training future leaders. The "reproduction" of wise, godly leaders is the responsibility of present-day leadership. As you lead, ask yourself, "Who in this group might mature into a leader, able to be used by God?" Deliberately encourage these people in their spiritual growth, in their personal disciplines and relationships, and in their identification and use of gifts. Invest in several individuals by praying for them and actively helping them develop the character and skills of a Christian leader.

The apostle Paul told Timothy, "If any one aspires to the office of bishop, he desires a noble task." Being a small group leader, too, is a noble and needed task. If you are willing to lead let me commend and encourage you.

Given the sizable task of leading, we must keep foremost in our minds that God gives his grace generously. At times you'll need a sense of humor. Maybe you've prepared a splendid Bible study, but for some inexplicable reason everyone falls asleep. Another time you may have scarcely prepared at all, yet the group is undeniably dynamic. It's the best meeting of the year!

God is mysteriously and graciously involved. The energy and responsiveness of group members is beyond our control. We can encourage their investment, but nothing can guarantee it.

How then do we come at our role? First we do our homework, but then we must laugh and relax. While we'd feel more secure if we were absolutely in control, the truth is that it's much more redemptive that God is in control. Luther wrote, "Were not the right man on our side, our striving would be losing." Our greatest strength and solace is simply Christ's grace and presence. It is his group, not ours.

Chapter 5
Sharing Leadership

A group's success does not depend solely on one designated leader. Whether the group jells and achieves its purpose is the responsibility of the entire group. It is simplistic and unrealistic to think in rigid categories of "leaders" and "followers." This is a disservice to all. It puts too much pressure on the designated leader—and too little on the other members. In truth everyone must cooperatively contribute to the group's growth and well-being.

Everyone a Leader
In chapter four we focused on the officiating leader within the small group, the designated leader. *The designated leader is the person appointed and recognized to be responsible for involving the group members in the desired life of the group.* For a group to function well, however, more leadership is required than the desig-

nated leader alone can provide. Without supplemental, informal leadership most groups would wither.

A fellowship group I've assisted for several years has been led by a presiding group of appointed leaders. They have furnished a great deal of positive impetus. Yet the "make-break" factor that has determined the success of the group year after year has been the unofficial, unappointed leaders. Last year Ray provided the crucial stimulation and organization for a strategic evangelistic effort. He was not a member of the group's steering committee. But having thought through the outreach idea and its potential impact, Ray presented his plan to the steering committee and they enthusiastically endorsed it.

Ray served as an informal leader. *An informal leader is any person who influences the group to meet needs and reach goals.* Every healthy small group has many such leaders. At different times and places in the life of a group, different members pick up various leadership functions. The most successful groups are those that help everyone in the group develop leadership skills.

Paul tells us in Ephesians 4:11-16 that leadership gifts have been distributed specifically "to equip the saints [all Christians], for the work of ministry, for building up the body of Christ, until we all attain to the unity of the faith and of the knowledge of the Son of God, to mature manhood, to the measure of the stature of the fulness of Christ" (vv. 12-13). The gifts have been distributed to all for the benefit of the collective body of Christ. Only when *all* the people in a small group (or a church or a fellowship) cooperatively contribute can significant spiritual growth take place.

If you are the designated leader, encourage members of the group to express their ideas, needs and understanding of what ought to be done. Overcome any sense of being threatened. The body of Christ is not supposed to have dictators or superstars. If openness, wide participation and group ownership can characterize your formal leadership, then you are being the type of servant-leader the body of Christ needs. And if you are not the formal leader of a small group, recognize that your insight is both valuable and required. Don't hang back assuming it's not your responsibility. It *is* your responsibility. God has gifted you, and your informal leadership and involvement are critical.

Every group needs a strong sense of unity and full participation. During the first few meetings it is essential that the formal leader direct the group to create this climate. He or she will need to initiate a lot of the group's activity and discussion at this early stage, until others in the group feel free to give their input and lead. Again, if the small group is entering its last few meetings, the formal leader may serve the well-being of the group by providing more initiative. At that point the group will need to express and reflect on the wide range of feelings they are experiencing (grief, disappointment, celebration) without being distracted by procedural demands.

During the bulk of the group's life, however, the designated leader can relax in initiative. In this middle phase the members operate together as a group, providing much more initiative themselves. At this point the group considers it "our" group, not "his" or "hers." All members contribute and lead in various ways. If this does not happen, the group will probably struggle and disintegrate. Figure 8 sketches these complementing periods of designated and informal initiative over the life span of a group.

Group unity and participation are encouraged as leadership flows from person to person, with the designated leader making sure that it happens. But there is a second way to increase the group's unity and commitment. That is for the leader to seek consensus on major decisions about the group's life. Of course, the leader can only do this if all the members talk about their feelings, needs and expectations. The leader's job is to help them feel comfortable and safe enough to talk.

It is appropriate for Bruce, as the formal leader, to express his

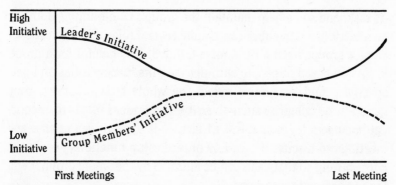

Figure 8. Initiative in a small group.

goals at the start. Everyone may agree, but it may be more tacit than expressed. So far, so good. But this is not consensus. John and Mary may be too afraid to voice opposition. Sue may be hesitant to say she is confused about the implications of several goals. How is the leader to know their thoughts when they don't speak? As time passes, the group will (or should!) be secure enough for members to voice their opinions, whether they agree with the leader or not. But the leader will have nonverbal clues as well. A lack of consensus may become all too evident as several members miss meetings, others arrive late or come unprepared, and others seem aloof or combative.

There is no substitute for consensus. The leader's best strategy is to get the group to determine as a group what commitments and goals they will make. Consensus must develop for "our" group to be established. In *Getting Together,* Em Griffin says that while consensus takes more time to achieve, greater commitment and higher quality decisions result. If you are the leader, you must be willing to risk pushing for consensus within the group.

Leadership Roles
Successful groups appoint people, whether formally or informally, to function in leadership roles. Some roles help the group achieve

its task, and some help maintain the group's community.[1] Both are necessary. Each member can handle several roles. Since most successful groups need all the roles fulfilled, it is helpful for a group to be composed of people with diverse gifts, personalities and perspectives. And, as groups reflect the whole body of Christ, they generally do comprise such diversity. The leader's role is to encourage members in their roles. In fact, it is a good idea after a few meetings to discuss the variety of leadership functions people are contributing so that each can be affirmed by the whole group. Let's look at some of these roles.

1. Timekeeper—helps the leader watch the time; keeps the group moving along if it stagnates; slows down the group when it's rushing.

2. Starter—initiates action in the group by suggesting objectives or tasks; helps the group implement plans.

3. Information and Opinion Seeker—requests statistics, information, news, possibilities and feelings from others in the group to facilitate discussion.

4. Information and Opinion Giver—provides statistics, information, news and possibilities that facilitate discussion; expands on what has already been said.

5. Active Listener—focuses attention on the person speaking; asks questions that elicit what others are thinking and feeling; seeks input from others.

6. Clarifier (or Communication Helper)—makes sure everyone understands clearly the discussion or expectations; helps avoid misunderstandings; facilitates dialog and interaction; eliminates vagueness and imprecision.

7. Summarizer—gathers the main emphasis of the group discussion and recapitulates it for the group; pulls the discussion together.

8. Diagnoser—identifies and analyzes the problems the group has in performing a task, reaching a goal or communicating well.

9. *Problem Solver*—works to resolve conflicts between members; increases sense of unity by facilitating open dialog and focusing on areas of agreement; helps group surmount problems and eliminate discrepancy; suggests compromise when appropriate.

10. *Coordinator*—demonstrates how different aspects of group discussion or group life interrelate; synchronizes action by members.

11. *Standard Setter*—works to achieve each member's compliance with group goals and procedures; helps monitor how well members are meeting standards.

12. *Reality Tester*—causes group to evaluate practicality of plans and expectations; discusses options; analyzes process and results; tactfully challenges the group on points of misunderstanding.

13. *Tension Reliever*—offers breaks from stress and strain by injecting humor or giving options for fun and enjoyable group activities.

14. *Encourager*—brings out the best from each; makes people feel included by affirming them, drawing them into the discussion, asking their viewpoint; helps build trust.

15. *Evaluator*—assesses how well the group is functioning or is accomplishing agreed-upon objectives; asks and assesses how group members are feeling about relationships, attitudes and expectations.

Balancing Group Life

The formal leader should evaluate the group's balance and consensus by regularly reviewing with the members their plans for community, nurture, worship and outreach. What are the goals and expectations? Are these plans being implemented? What adjustments need to be made in plans or practice?

It's easy for members who mesh together well to become enthralled with one another. The community thrives but the outreach shrivels. Or a group that likes to study may neglect relationships, and, as a result, a sense of Christian community never emerges. These components need to be creatively held in tension. A good leader will help the group stride toward them all.

Undoubtedly, if you are the formal leader, you will be faced with many dilemmas. Sometimes you'll succeed marvelously; other times you will be faced with too much to handle. What do you do when Karen and Jim are not participating in the group? Or when, while you are conducting a calm Bible study, Jeff begins to sob? Do you go on or stop? What do you do when the community time has used up all the nurture time? How do you help a group that seems hesitant to reach out beyond the group? Your commitment and the group's to the four basic components of a small group can help you sort some of these issues.

Group balance may also be measured by using a grid evaluating three planes of a group's life: (1) the needs of individual members, (2) the needs of a task and (3) the need for group maintenance. Every person in the group, including the leader, has personal needs. The needs can be anything—spiritual, social, psychological, intellectual and emotional. For instance, we all need, in the emotional sphere, love, security, recognition, freedom from guilt, and new experiences. Obviously, no group is going to meet all these needs all of the time, or even most of the time. But people do expect that *some* needs will be met. If they aren't, members will begin to drop out.

Second, the group has a task, its reasons for meeting. Perhaps your group set out to study the Gospel of Mark, to support one another and to evangelize a neighborhood. If the outreach to the neighborhood is forgotten or displaced, members may feel frustrated. Everyone needs to know what the tasks are, to agree that they are worthwhile and then to work to make them happen.

Third is the need for group maintenance. Just as individuals have needs that must be met, so does the group as a whole. The behind-the-scenes activity of the leader in making arrangements and caring for details saves the group from needless frustration. Ample time for fun, conflict resolution, care and evaluation must also be allowed. These promote the group's sense of community and heighten the sense of a common purpose.

These three needs must find balance. Individuals' needs must be met. The task needs to be accomplished. The group needs to develop a corporate sense of satisfaction. At times, one need will take priority. Initially the need to build community will take priority over the task. As individual needs begin to be met, more time can be invested in the task. There are no hard and fast rules. The formal leader must pray, risk and lead, striving to guide the group into a balanced life. Lord willing, the entire group will catch the vision.

Chapter 6
The Life Cycle of a Group

"*Our group began so* well. I thought I had finally found a group that would meet my needs. Then people stopped coming. Our sharing became superficial. The whole group seemed to fall apart. I'm wondering about the Christian commitment of these people.*"

These words are repeated time after time as groups start and then flounder. Members experience failure, rejection and anger; they hurt and yearn for healing. For leaders these same feelings are heightened, so that they may hesitate to ever lead a group again. How does this disaster happen?

Ironically, many groups end just at the point when they are about to begin. If the members knew more about group dynamics and the normal changes that occur in groups as time passes, they would know to hang on when the going gets tough. Tension, lack of commitment and even conflict between members might launch the group into a new phase of growth together and in Christ.

Groups are not static organisms. They have a life cycle from birth through infancy and adolescence to adulthood and, sometimes, death. Leaders especially need to realize this. Knowing the pattern will help them accept their group wherever it is and press on for further growth and fulfillment. The basic cycle can be divided into four stages: *exploration, transition, action* and *termination.*

Exploration

Bob glanced at his watch. 5:00 P.M. He hurried out of his office and down the stairs. He didn't want to meet Ann late since tonight was the first meeting of their small group. For some time he had been looking forward to this meeting. It might be just what he needed to make God more than an idea to him. Ann's words kept haunting him: "I need someone to take spiritual leadership in this family."

Maybe getting together with others would be the trick he needed for the truth of Christianity to come alive to him. He knew little about the other couples who would be there. What would the group be like? Would others think he wasn't a Christian if he shared his problem with Ann? What would the group's goals be? What kind of format would it follow? Bob was hesitant and anxious but hopeful. Because Jeff and Sally Henderson had personally invited them, he felt reasonably sure that others were interested in him.

Think back to the last group you were a member of. What was it like? What feelings did you have at first? What questions were running through your mind? Although they may not have been the same as Bob's, your questions probably involved one key issue— *inclusion.* During the exploration stage we evaluate whether we feel a part of the group in three areas: people, power and purpose.

People—Do I feel included in this group? Do I want to include the others in my life? Can I trust the others enough to risk expressing my true thoughts and feelings?

Power—Will I be included in the decision-making process of the group? Will my ideas be included in the discussion?

Purpose—How will the group use its time? What kind of commitments will the group ask me to make? Will the group meet my personal needs?

Most new group members come expecting their needs to be met. Although they feel somewhat anxious, they are usually willing to give an initial downpayment of trust to the leader and other members of the group during the exploration stage—which is why groups usually begin with a flourish.

The designated leader's initiative is key in this stage. The leader must help members answer the people, purpose and power questions. Without such leadership most groups do not move on but remain superficial, lacking in commitment and direction.

Look again at figure 7 on page 31, and notice how the plans for weeks one and two take into account the tenuous feelings of the group at its start. The Bible study answers in capsule form Bob's question about the group's purpose—it will meet for nurture, worship, community and mission. *What* it will do more specifically and *how* it will go about it the whole group will have to decide later on. Notice that worship the first week is brief and puts pressure on no one, since the group members are still strangers to one another. Under "Community," the leader initiates a way to break down those feelings of being a stranger by serving popcorn (food always helps!) and using the "Warm Up" exercise.

Looking at the plan for week two, still at the exploration stage, you can see how the leader gradually builds on the growing mutual trust in each of the four elements. Take a moment to look ahead to Community Resources, where on pages 164-65 "Who Am I?" and "Warm Up" are explained. Notice that they appear with a whole group of exploration exercises so that a leader can easily choose the appropriate one. The other exercises, too, are grouped by stage to help you lead your group into deepening fellowship and purpose.

So Bob's group is off to a solid start. But it is a naive leader who assumes that these early meetings are all they seem to be. For most groups some rocky times lie ahead. Members will continue to wrestle with their own commitment to the others, with the purposes of the group and with their place and power within the group. This stage is called transition.

Transition

"I think we ought to get out of the group now," confided Bob. "I mean, it's fun to be with Jeff and Sally, but I don't think they are aware of how important an open group is to us. Besides, the Woolards are always late, and it seems like they can't talk about anything but church problems. Why can't we talk about something more *personal?*"

Ann was at a loss. She too had hoped this group would meet their needs, but now she wasn't sure. Who was really making the decisions? Should they confront the Hendersons, complain to the whole group—or just leave and look somewhere else?

Sound familiar? It should. This kind of discussion goes on behind the scenes of many groups. The issue is conflict, conflict in those same three areas (of people, power and purpose) that tell us whether we are included in the group. After the group is under way and members no longer strangers, personality differences may surface. Or the group's purposes may not be meeting *my* needs. Or I may disagree with the functioning leader.

We are often afraid of conflict. Yet conflict is inevitable. We cannot get away from it. We must learn to deal with it in a healthy and godly way. This is what transition is all about.

The honeymoon (exploration) is over. The group is beginning to move to a new level of maturity. It is true that a wholesome exploration period will ward off many potential conflicts, but conflict of some sort is still inevitable and, in fact, even healthy.

People—In our experience, the basic element which allows a group to succeed is this: no matter what the group's task is, all members take their relationship to one another seriously. They must know and be known by each other. They must feel that the leader cares for and respects them. Members must experience a sense of belonging—of "rightness," comfortableness and security in the group. When conflict, whatever the cause, breaks down this aura of acceptingness, the best help comes by opening up communication.

God desires good communication with us, and we do well as his creatures to look at his model. Three principles of his communication with us can guide us.

First, God cares so much that he goes out of his way to speak. As the writer to the Hebrews puts it, "In many and various ways God spoke of old to our fathers by the prophets; but in these last days he has spoken to us by a Son" (1:1-2). God sticks with us until we hear him. We need to do the same for each other. Bob and Ann need to speak out their disappointments and yearnings, lovingly, making sure that they are understood before they leave feeling hurt or rejected. This is true for every member of the group. (Doing "A Round," page 170, could open discussion for the Bobs and Anns in your group.)

Second, God's communication is listener-centered. God cared so much about our understanding him that he became like us. The Incarnation shows how God was more concerned about his listeners than he was in just winning an argument or demonstrating his power. Good leaders will put themselves in the other's place, and help others do the same.

Third, God becomes involved with his listeners. Jesus involved himself in the lives of those he wanted to understand his message. He touched the leper. He allowed a woman to kiss his feet and wipe them with her hair. Jesus' communication was more than words.

We need to learn not only more about verbal communication but about our whole style of communicating with others.[1]

Power—During exploration the designated leader took on much of the decision-making power on issues of when, where, what and how long. At the transition stage members want to have more say in what the group does. They want to know how decisions are made and to have more influence in the group. A wise leader hands more and more power to the group as time passes (see figure 8, p. 53). The goal is to develop a group that sees itself as "our group" and not just the leader's group.

Purpose—No small group can meet every need of every person. If the group is to succeed, however, it must meet some of the needs of all its participants. During transition the purpose of the group takes center stage. If the group cannot agree on and articulate its purpose, it may dissolve.

Many of the purposes the leader set for the group in exploration are now being questioned by other members. Bob and Ann are uncertain whether the purposes of the group are meeting their needs. Their questions can threaten the leader, who feels criticized. If he becomes defensive, however, he discourages openness at best, and dissolves the group at worst. As the Hendersons sense Bob and Ann's concerns, they must communicate that they are glad for Bob and Ann's honesty and openness, and that they are not threatened by the negative feedback. By the transition stage, however, the group is beginning to "own" itself. When any member of the group expresses discontent, the *group* needs to respond, not just the original leader.

One way to clarify purposes and to resolve the tensions of transition is to develop a group covenant. A covenant is a written statement that helps group members put love into action. What goes into such a statement? Think of a covenant in terms of these four *c's:* content, commitments, context and climate.

Content is what we do with the time in our group. It will, of course, be a balance of worship, nurture, community and mission. But the covenant would spell out more specifically what might be done; that is, study the Bible, eat, pray, sing, read a book. Our church small group has the motto "May God be with us 'til we *eat* again"!

Commitments tell what we expect each member to do as a part of the group: attend all the meetings, come prepared, be on time, pray for one another, be willing to share honestly, meet one-to-one outside the group.

Context answers the who, what, where, when questions. Who is a member? Is the group open to new members or not? How long do we meet? At whose home?

Climate concerns the tone of the group. Are we to be open, honest, warm? Are we expected to share our feelings or is it okay just to talk about ideas?

Many groups get frustrated as they write their covenants. Conflicting expectations and commitments can cause members to feel angry. Better to work it all out ahead of time so that no one is disappointed when private expectations don't get met. You can't have one kind of climate if the commitments or content call for another. If a group decides to meet only for Bible study as content, then no one should be expecting the kind of sociality that comes with eating together. If the commitment is to "come if you can," then the climate will be more casual and superficial.

For most groups these four *c's* must fit together to facilitate meeting group members' expectations. The covenanting clears the way for harmony between purpose and expectation, between what you intend to do and accomplish in the group and what you expect to get out of it. When the group has shaped its covenant it usually moves into the *action stage*. Notice that formulating the covenant is the mission activity for the sample plan in figure 7 (p. 31). Those six weeks saw the group through exploration and transition. Now it's ready to work.

Action

A key word for the action stage is "freedom." Group members are free in several areas. *Free* to be themselves. They know they are accepted and therefore do not need to wear masks. *Free* to commit themselves to the group covenant because they have a vested interest in the goals of the group. *Free* to talk openly because they know they have been forgiven by God and come with the others as needy yet expectant people.

This is the time when the group will accomplish most of its activity in mission. You have reached an important milestone as a leader. You can now allow the group to have its own life. Others will be leading because they will feel free to use their gifts. You will still need to help the group keep its vision, perhaps reminding them of their goals. In a sense you will lead by encouraging members to lead.[2]

We have seen groups move in and out of the action stage within a year. Sometimes members' concerns and problems put the group back into transition. This is all normal. The group will move back into action as they deal with the issue at hand.

This is an exciting period for everyone. It is the time in the group that will produce memories for all. We who write this book have lived in several areas of the world and been involved in numerous small groups. Our memories from these groups are what convince us that they are worth the risk of personal failure and hurt. The small group "in action" is the church in action, doing its mission of extending God's love to one another and to the world.

Termination

The final stage is termination. Some church groups end only to restart with a new agenda or a new commitment to the old. But every group has an ending of some sort, and participants should realize this from the start. Termination is often a hard time for groups. It's hard to say good-by.

I remember when I left Boston after serving as a campus minister for six years. I wanted to just slip out of town. I didn't want anyone to make a fuss over me. I now realize that this was unfair to myself and to others. Students at Harvard literally had to track me down to give me a gift.

In termination a small group celebrates and commemorates what the group and individuals in the group have meant to each one. It gives us an opportunity to deal with many of the emotions that we feel as a group ends. Good termination is like a good funeral: it helps us work through the emotions we feel to see something end.

Our church group ends twice a year. We sometimes have started again with the very same group, but at least we have had the opportunity to express to one another what the group has meant to us. We have also been able to evaluate the life of the group, which helps us as we restart. We may start again with some new members, some old.

During termination the designated leader must again take initiative. You need to help members resolve their feelings. The conclusion should be seen as the end of a commitment to meet in a certain way to do certain things. And the commitment to each other will no doubt be different—but it will still be there. After all, your small group was only a particular focus of the whole church, and in the whole body of Christ we remain related, committed to care. You'll still be seeing lots of each other, still worshiping together in the whole-church meetings.

As the designated leader you thus serve by making the termination a pleasant occasion for everyone. Suggest that each one share or bring gifts so that feelings are warm and positive. You'll know the group has succeeded if everyone is eager to be a part of a group again.

Knowing something about a group's normal life cycle can help leaders. But let me caution you. These stages are *de*scriptive and not *pre*scriptive for small groups. That is, they describe groups, they don't say how they should go. Leaders should not try to force their groups through these stages. However, you should not be surprised when, for instance, conflicts arise. Reconciliation toward unity in Christ is the work of God in his church. It is also his work in church small groups. May Christian fellowship become such a reality in your group that the world will notice and say, "See how they love one another!"

Chapter 7

How to Begin Small Groups and Make Them Multiply

So you are ready to join a small group. Great! But your church doesn't have any. What's more, your pastor has encouraged *you* to begin one! Where do you start?

If you are starting a small group in your church, you will in fact be the designated leader, at least until the group chooses another. As such you will need, long before the first meeting, to think through several essential issues:

1. What purpose do you hope the group will serve?
2. Who and how many should be invited to join?
3. What should happen in your *first* small group meeting?
4. How can your group grow so that it ultimately spawns new groups?

Clarifying the Group's Purpose

As we have already seen, the leader helps *the group* to decide on its purpose and task. But the group can only do this in its transition stage. Until that time it is you, the leader, who have to determine its reason for being. Some groups start and then flounder simply because no one knows why the group exists!

We earlier defined small groups in the church as people joined together to meet needs and to do the ministry of the church. One major aspect of the church's ministry is to meet one another's needs, to help each other reflect God's glory more brilliantly. So start by asking, What personal and spiritual needs do you and your friends at church have that could be met within a small group?

Do any of you need to grow into a deeper understanding of Scripture or in seeing how to apply it to your lives? Perhaps you are struggling in witnessing to some non-Christian friends at work or in your neighborhood, and a small group could focus on learning personal evangelism skills. Perhaps you simply need encouragement to live a Christ-centered life.

Spiritual growth usually occurs as people have the opportunity to interact together in God's Word, drawing out personal applications that will help each one mature in Christ. Therefore, one part of your group's purpose will be to discover and meet needs within each other through Bible study, prayer and application of the Word of God to your daily circumstances.

Perhaps you are wanting to start a small group because you have in mind a ministry or outreach that will take a group to accomplish. If you can find like-minded Christians to join you, the other elements of group life will come later.

Look around within your church and community. What needs exist that your small group could help fill? Discuss possibilities for mission with group members or potential group members.

One church in Washington, D.C., has a network of "mission" groups that are involved in fulfilling different kinds of mission or specific ministries. The ministries range from leading a discipleship-training school for new members, to serving the urban poor, to running a coffee house. Your outreach or service beyond the group need not be elaborate. If group members are deeply involved in personal ministries, the group may choose as its mission to help strengthen and encourage each of the members for their ministry.

Jim and Susan were interested in starting a group that would reach out to friends in their neighborhood who were unsure of their faith. They shared their idea with some of the church members in their neighborhood. Their plan was to meet with a group of three to six couples who would weekly study Scripture that focused primarily on family relationships.

The group helped each other verbalize their faith, and prayed for each other's witness. In between meetings several members shared with one another what Christ was doing in their lives as they spent time with neighbors in various activities and witness opportunities. After six weeks of study together, they sponsored the Dobson film series on the family and invited their neighborhood friends to participate. They showed the films every other week in the community center of the development where they all lived. With Jim and Susan's preliminary thinking and the group's more precise planning, the group succeeded in its purpose of extending the good news.

Another group began primarily as a nurture group, the first in the church. The members were so excited about their experience of growing faith and love that they wanted to help others in their church have a similar opportunity. Eventually they began to view their small group as a training ground from which new groups could emerge. Various members were sent out by the group to pioneer fledgling groups.

Inviting People

Who should join the group depends on what the group's purpose is. Are you aiming, for example, at starting a group whose primary purpose is to nurture and disciple its members? Then look for those who would be most eager for such a commitment. Or are you like Jim and Susan, already having a specific ministry or outreach in mind, just looking for people to share your vision and task with? Consider also age, sex and geography—where people live. Geography was key in Jim and Susan's purpose.

How many people should be in a small group? To facilitate communication and to keep everyone directly involved, limit the size of your group. Groups of eight to ten people are best. Groups larger than this usually wind up with two kinds of members—those who are very active and involved, and those who are basically spectators, watching from the sidelines but not much involved. So invite about ten people, including yourself, to start and see how many come. (If your group grows beyond about twelve members, you may want to think about starting another group.)

However you decide whom to invite, you'll want to talk personally with each potential member. One-to-one talks in which you share your excitement and a little about what you see as the group's purpose are best. Show genuine interest in them. Discover what they are thinking or feeling about their spiritual life. Your openness about your own walk with Jesus will help set a tone of openness and trust.

As you discover common concerns and needs, share how involvement in a small group could help meet those needs. If you have been in a group before that was meaningful and enriching, tell about it. Share your excitement. Often as I talk with potential members about a new group I say, "I believe God wants to do something in us and through us that he has chosen not to do in any other way. Out of our commitment to each other we will become more human and more perfect in Christ." Emphasize that our involvement together in the Word of God is the primary way that God changes us.

As you are talking with prospective members, you may be aware of their gifts which, if exercised in the group, would make for a much stronger small group. Encourage them and let them know that they are wanted and needed in the small group.

Finally, as you talk personally with each potential member, put him or her on your prayer list. Ask God to select those whom he wants to be involved in your small group.

The process of sharing and inviting potential members may take weeks. Before the first "official" small group meeting some small group leaders plan a social evening in which potential members can meet each other and discuss expectations and hopes for small group involvement in their church. This could be a potluck dinner or picnic. It should be informal. Toward the end of the evening you may want to decide when and where your first "real" group meeting is to be. Perhaps you could also decide how often the group will meet.

Some groups choose to meet weekly. There are definite advantages to this, as you will see each other often enough to be supportive of each other. Others, unable to make a weekly commitment, meet every other week. To meet less frequently than this is self-defeating. You simply will not be able to build sufficient community within the group if meetings are too sporadic.

Meeting for the First Time
The first meeting is crucial. The setting and atmosphere of the meeting must be right. Choose a room that is free from distractions. Arrange seats so that everyone can have good eye contact with everyone else.

Your attitude as a leader will set the tone of the evening. Although you may feel nervous, having prepared ahead will help you relax and feel more confident. As people arrive, welcome them. If people do not know each other very well, you may want to provide name tags.

At this first meeting you as leader should initiate. You might divide the evening into four segments: (1) informal conversation;

(2) brief worship, leading into structured sharing; (3) Bible study; and (4) mission discussion.

Begin with a time of informal conversation before the meeting comes to order. This may be a good time to serve refreshments. After this informal time, making sure all the members have arrived, call the meeting to order. One way to begin is to lead the group in singing several familiar choruses. (If there is a guitarist or pianist in the group, you could prearrange for accompaniment. If not, sing anyway.)

Help members focus on God's presence in the group. You might give a sentence definition of worship: "Worship is acknowledging God's presence and fellowship with us." Follow this definition with a brief sentence prayer in which *you* acknowledge his presence.

This moves the group into the next phase, structured sharing. Members will need to get to know each other. Ample suggestions on how to do this are in this book's resource section under "Community." You'll be looking, of course, for those activities intended for the exploration stage. Focus on exercises that are self-descriptive, for example, those that ask members to describe things like their favorite color or their favorite vacation spot. Most of this sharing should be done in twos and threes.

You could draw the sharing time to a close by turning the group focus, through pointed questions, to the Bible study topic. For example, if you are to study a passage like Acts 2:42-47, ask, "As Christians, what should be the priorities in our life together?"

Now you are ready for the third segment of your meeting, Bible study. This study should be shorter at the first meeting than usual. Thirty minutes on a passage like Acts 2:42-47 probably will be sufficient. Introduce your study with something that will capture interest, and be sure to conclude solidly as well.[1] Interest will probably be strong as you discuss how to apply the passage to your personal and group lives.

The final segment of your first meeting should help the members focus on mission. Mission is, as we will discuss in chapter eleven, sharing in word and deed the good news of Christ's love to people in need. It is especially important at this first meeting that you build some expectations in group members of reaching out beyond themselves to share Christ's love in word and deed with people in need. You may ask members to spend a few minutes in prayer together for non-Christian friends. Or you may want to introduce your group to one of your church's missionaries, telling something of his or her ministry and needs, so that the group can pray.

Conclude the meeting by praying for each other. Share prayer requests and perhaps pray in pairs for each other. Do not forget to decide where and when your next meeting will be.

Multiplying Groups

As the group first begins, members have a basic need to develop community that outweighs, for the time, the group's focus on worship, nurture or mission. Therefore you will probably spend more time at first in activities which facilitate your getting to know each other. Some groups decide to lay aside extended periods of time in which this becomes the primary focus. For example, you may choose to have a meal together before the meeting begins for the first few weeks of your small group's life, and then once a month after that.

As time passes, however, all the elements will come into balance and the group will indeed meet needs and do the work of the church. You will discover God's Spirit powerfully present. And when he is released in us and through us, the result is always spiritual and numerical growth.

As the group grows spiritually, members will be reaching out to others that they want to see growing as well. The tendency at this point is to simply bring in more and more new members. The closeness that has come in the group is so powerful that no one wants to see the group divide.

Don't fall into this trap! As new members join and the group expands in numbers beyond twelve, the closeness felt when the group had eight to ten members will be lost anyway. You cannot have the same depth of relationship with twelve to fifteen people that you can with eight. You will need to multiply your group by dividing.

One of the best ways is to select several people from your group to be "pioneers." Paul and Barnabus were selected by the church at Antioch. They were both capable teachers, loved by those in the church. Their ministry was so powerful that the Christians at Antioch were made aware that the blessings which they had received from the gospel were not just for them personally but for others as well. Therefore, the Holy Spirit directed them to send off two of their finest teachers that others might hear. The Christians at Antioch continued in their care for Paul and Barnabus as they heard how God was blessing others through them.

Your group will discover this excitement when you are ready to select members to go and raise up daughter small groups. Whether it ever does, however, depends largely on how the group starts out. The first meeting is key in setting the tone for all that comes.

Good things do come in small groups, and you've chosen a worthy task if you've decided to form one. With the initial hurdle of the first meeting over, and with continuing care and prayer for your group's spiritual health, you are on your way.

In part two we turn to look in depth at the four elements that will make your small group a good one. Nurture, worship, community and mission are the backbone of the small group. The chapters that follow will demonstrate how key they are for Christian life.

Part 2
Four Key Ingredients

Chapter 8
Nurture

Heading for small group leader training one night, I noticed I had left my notes at the office. I went back for them, mumbling, "If one more thing goes wrong . . ." I was greeted at the church by the pastor: "You're late!" Obviously it was going to be a great evening.

My teaching didn't go well. Someone in my group talked too much, others not enough. The evening was one big frustration.

I hadn't eaten supper or lunch, and I felt hungry. By the time I got home I had a headache. Munching an apple, I thought over the evening. The headache lessened. I ate some crackers; now I felt fine! I understood: my body had been out of fuel. I needed food. We need nutrients in our bodies both to perform well and to keep emotional balance.

Our spiritual lives are like that, too. The spiritual body needs nutritious food to bear the fruit that shows we are Christ's disciples

(Jn 15:8). Your small group needs to be nurtured. Leland Eliason, a professor at Bethel Seminary in St. Paul, put it this way: "Those who give into the pressures of ministry by failing to study will run dry; those who give into the pressure of study by not being involved with people will become distant."

Jesus saw his disciples' need for spiritual food. He concentrated his teaching on twelve disciples, and then he gave the Holy Spirit to continue teaching them so that they would continue to abide in him and bear fruit (Jn 14:25-26; 15:1-11). Disciples for generations to come would grow as they remembered Jesus and obeyed his words.

The Acts 2 Pattern
We also want disciples in our churches to grow and bear fruit. How can small groups nurture this development? Acts 2:42 tells us how the community in the early church was nurtured for ministry. "They devoted themselves to the apostles' teaching and to the fellowship, to the breaking of bread and to prayer" (NIV). Let me begin at the end of this verse, with prayer, and move to the beginning.

"They devoted themselves to . . . prayer."

Prayer becomes part of us because God has touched our spirit with his own. He has called us into relationship with himself. In prayer we enter the privileges and responsibilities of that relationship.

Prayer nurtures our worship and love of God. It also nurtures our sense of involvement in those things for which we pray. If prayer changes things, the one "thing" it changes most is the one who prays.

Reading prayers like Paul's in Ephesians gives us a strong sense of God's greatness and power in life. Because God is love and because he is powerful, we turn to him—to worship, to intercede, to ask forgiveness. We turn in prayer to the one who as King of kings and Lord of lords has loved and redeemed us. He cares for all the world. He has been a faithful God in the past. He will continue to be so. He has invited us to commune with him. No wonder so many prayers have words of worship in them! And as the Spirit brings us into prayer, we are fed for a deeper relationship with God.

Take time in your group for silence before you pray, time to realize who God is. Let God speak to you of his love for you, his power, his faithfulness. He dwells in us and so speaks to us as we speak with him. Listen to him. Let him nurture your spirit and then respond together. You will find your group moving quickly to worship.

The Spirit also nurtures our sense of responsibility in prayer. It is hard to commit myself to pray for someone without allowing myself to be the answer to that prayer. If I pray that a woman may hear of Jesus Christ, am I willing to be the one who speaks to her? If I pray for the alleviation of hunger in the world, am I willing to do without in order to give to that end? When I pray I must ask myself, Do I want God to answer so that I don't have to get involved? Or am I desiring to see God work in situations, in people—possibly through me.

"Thy kingdom come, Thy will be done" (Mt 6:10). Christ ushered in a new kingdom. His followers were to continue the presence of that kingdom "on earth as it is in heaven." Prayer reminds us that we have a part in doing his will, not just in talking about it. The Spirit cultivates concerns in us so that we may bring them to the Almighty, and also so that we may be part of Christ's body bringing his kingdom to earth. Our prayer together opens us up for God to speak to us about his concerns and for us to commit ourselves to his will.

"They devoted themselves to . . . the breaking of bread."

It is likely that the breaking of bread in the early Christian church was part of the agape feast, the communal meal. In this act of fellowship with one another, believers are drawn to remember Jesus not only as he shared this feast with the apostles, but more as he gave himself for our redemption. That remembrance leads us to worship, but it also reminds us that the Giver of the feast is our nourishment for life. Communion celebrates our living Savior. The breaking of bread is a means whereby together as his body we experience God's power for abundant life. His redeeming presence nurtures us in his gifts of grace, encouraging us to live as his followers.

Communion reminds us, too, of the common life and faith we share in Christ. Christ binds us together. In his life and death he sustains us as a community to be committed to one another, working through differences, caring for needs, struggling to understand Christ's lordship in our life.

Your small group may want to eat meals together for times of fellowship and being nurtured by God's provision for us. You can also ask your pastor into a small group meeting so that you can partake of the Lord's Supper together. In some churches it would be quite appropriate to break bread just as your own group. Or your group can sit together in church on Communion Sunday to eat and drink together at Christ's feast given for you.

"They devoted themselves . . . to the fellowship."

Church fellowship was based on the Christians' unity with the Lord and with each other. The book of Acts emphasizes how they shared property. Personal resources were given for the good of other believers.

What resources do we have to offer each other? Probably many. Giving, whether material (money, food), emotional (caring, listening) or intellectual (insights, knowledge, reactions), nurtures the growth and development of the whole body. The material needs we meet not only nurture the body or alleviate worries but provide for a sense of well-being, a sense that "someone cares about me." Christ reaches out to people through his body to meet needs.

We all have emotional needs as well. As we listen to people, affirm them, take initiative with them, we once again offer them the love of Christ. This alleviates immediate needs as well as nurtures a positive self-concept, that "God loves you as you are, his child."

Mark came to our small group meeting more quiet and withdrawn than usual. He had had his yearly job evaluation that afternoon. It had not been particularly negative, but neither had he received any outstanding affirmation. He felt like a failure. He didn't know what else to do since he thought what he did at work was what he could do best. Our group could not change his job evaluation or Mark's attitude toward the evaluation. But we could listen. We could care. We heard his disappointments and fears. We affirmed him in the things we had seen him do well and in the things we appreciated about him. After a time he was able to relax with some spark of knowing that his worth was not equated with his job review. After being fed by his brothers and sisters in Christ, he was able to withdraw from his thoughts about the day and be nurtured by the Word of God.

When we feel good about ourselves, we are open to new input. We are free to grow. We can absorb new challenges and thoughts which lead to growth in our discipleship. At times these new ideas may be hard for us to understand, but one strength small group sharing has is that we take time to understand others. Individuals in a small group will often have varied perspectives on issues, even on the Bible, and we can learn and grow from their different backgrounds and experiences. We stop putting God and his ways of working in a box. We find ourselves knowing him in new ways.

Another way the small group nurtures its members is through the affirmation and encouragement of one another. As we spend time together in a variety of settings (study, sharing, fun, work), we see each other's strengths and weaknesses. We can encourage each other to keep growing and stretching. Because we knew Mark, we could affirm his gifts and strengths, concretely and honestly, when he was discouraged.

Sometimes we take what we do well for granted and fail to see it as a gift God has given us for serving the body of Christ. Feedback from a small group can make us aware of our gifts and alert us to use them for God, as he intended.

Suzanne told Bill, "You really listen to people and seem to be perceptive in hearing more than words."

"Well, thank you, but doesn't everybody?" Bill asked.

"We are supposed to, but not many seem to listen as well and respond as sensitively as you do." And that was true. But he had never seen his behavior as unusual.

Helping Bill see his gift as a gift supported him as a needed member of our group. Our message was, "No, not everyone can do what you do, and not everyone can be who you are. You are unique; we need you, and the church needs you to exercise your gift." Small groups work for the upbuilding of each other and for the work of ministry (Eph 4:12). True Christian fellowship cultivates growth in others as we make ourselves and our resources available.

"They devoted themselves to the apostles' teaching."

Jesus taught by word and example how his followers should live and what they should believe. These earliest believers passed on Jesus' teaching so that others might believe (Jn 17:20). They also studied and passed on the Old Testament, particularly those parts pertaining to Jesus.

Today we find this teaching gathered in the Old and New Testaments, the Bible. It is our main source of nurture. Our faith and lives develop and grow as we study the Scripture. Our life together is also fed and nourished by the Word of God. The Scriptures point us to Christ the Lord. As we abide in him our fruit bearing reaches others.

How can you guide your group into the study of Scripture so that they can be energized to bear fruit? The role of a Bible study leader includes (1) preparing the study, (2) introducing the study, (3) facilitating discussion questions and (4) summarizing the discussion. Let's look at each of these.

Preparing the Study

Preparation is key to being at ease with your small group in Bible study. Through it we feed ourselves so we can teach others to feast on the Word of God. We prepare *not* so we can teach, expound our findings or actively control the group. We prepare so we know the material and can guide others to see main truths. Preparation helps us keep the discussion on track so we get at major teachings of the passage. Other topics may be interesting but are better coffee-time topics. Preparing gives us a handle on what questions we should use to move us toward the main points in the study.

Try using a Bible study guide for your group. Many good ones are available (see listing in chapter fourteen, Nurture Resources). Guides give direction and focus to your study. Besides, writing a good study yourself takes lots of time.

A guide does not negate the need for preparation. You still need a strong grasp of the content of the passage and the direction of the study. The following steps will help you prepare a Bible study for your small group (see also suggestions for preparing and leading a Bible study in chapter thirteen, pages 140-41):

1. Get some background information. This will probably come from two sources. First, the book of the Bible you are studying: Observe main themes, repeated words, main characters and principal divisions or changes in action, and so on. Figure out what the context of the passage is. Second, other sources: Glean historical background from other books of the Bible (for example, read Acts 16 when studying Philippians) and Bible dictionaries.

2. Study the passage first without your guide. First, observe main people, places, causes and effects, repeated words. Ask what is significant about what you have observed. What seems to be the

main theme or topic of this passage? ("God's love is our source of strength in difficult times.") Then ask, What meaning does this passage have for people today? in my small group? for our church life? (See #4 below.)

3. Take your study guide and work through the questions. Now that you know the passage well and understand it, you can see how the questions help discover the truth of this passage.

4. Prepare your goals. What is the meaning of the passage for your group? What truth does it have for your members? Write out a goal you may have for studying this passage; for example, "to develop more open sharing in our group," or "to see God's power for us that we may begin some group outreach."

5. Use a series of "discovery" questions. Often in our study we go immediately to asking, "What do you think about this?" or "How does this passage apply to us?" When we ask interpretation and application questions too quickly, we may miss the main point because we haven't looked at the passage long enough. The three steps of Bible study are *observation, interpretation* and *application.* We must observe important facts before we move on to ask why such-and-such is significant, why such-and-such is important in our life.

Look at the questions in your study guide. Which ones are observation? interpretation? application? Which questions are key in leading to the main truth? Remember, you need all three types of questions to get to the heart of the passage. Make sure you intersperse the questions both to keep discussion active and to get to the application in case you run short of time. You may have a couple of observation and interpretation questions and then an application, followed by another series of observation, interpretation, application. (See the Acts 2 study under Nurture Resources, pp. 154-55.)

6. Develop an introduction which will bring people into the study. Focus their attention on the passage, the situation, the

feelings of the people involved (see below).

7. Be praying for yourself and your group as you prepare. Ask God to help all to be open to the teaching in his Word. Pray that you would be free to lead others and open to new insights they may have.

Introducing the Study

In your introduction you want to catch people's attention and involve them in the study right away. These openers give the idea:

"There are so many groups within Christianity. They often have different ways to worship, varying doctrines, and opposing views on issues. Tonight we are going to look at what is basic in Christianity and ties us all together. Let's turn to Ephesians 1."

"Jesus interacted with people from all walks of life. Think of an area in your life where you aren't so sure you'd want Jesus to see you operate—a business deal, treatment of your in-laws, attitudes toward the poor . . . or the rich. How would Jesus interact with us at each point? Let's see how Jesus met a woman whose behavior was not exactly Christlike" *(introducing John 4)*.

If the passage is a dialog, suggest that members take roles and read aloud. Or you may want to set the scene (beside a fishing lake or whatever) and describe it for the group as they close their eyes to imagine it. (You could use some of your background information.) Your introduction should help people think, "I want to know more about that!" "Let's get at it!" "That is an important question!"

Facilitating Discussion

As the leader, you don't have to have all the answers or be able to hold forth for twenty minutes on how reconciliation relates to propitiation. You are asked to help others discover biblical insights. To do this, you will ask questions, respond encouragingly, summarize periodically and offer your insights when appropriate.

Of course, you'll have help from the whole group as they all warm up to sharing leadership, as we saw in chapter five.

You will find it helpful to begin your group with the following ground rules:

1. Approach the Bible fresh and open to learning, just as you would any good book.

2. Avoid leaning on information from outside sources; let the text speak for itself.

3. Expect the text, not the leader, to answer questions.

4. Stay in the passage under consideration.

5. Strive for balanced participation.

State these guidelines to the group at your first study and repeat them periodically over the weeks that follow. These give the group an idea of expectations and also serve as a foundation if you need to confront a problem later (such as tangents).

Here are some other suggestions to help in facilitating your discussion:

1. Ask questions, don't lecture. Offer some of your insights when helpful. Do not, however, answer your own questions when there is silence. Reword a question if needed. You do not need to share everything you have found in your preparation. People will not find everything in a thirty- to forty-minute discussion when it took you two hours of preparation to discover it! Ask questions that lead to more than a yes or no answer. You may need to reword a question in your guide.

2. Let more than one person answer a question by opening the floor to others: "What else do the rest of you see?" "What can others add to that?"

3. Acknowledge answers by listening carefully. Either verbally or nonverbally affirm a good answer: "Yes!" "Right!" "Thanks, that was helpful." Nodding, smiling, good eye contact—all these encourage participation.

4. Include everyone. You may want to have quieter members

read the passage or list the people mentioned. One reason to study as a group is to get input from the group—that is, everyone. Be sure everyone understands this. For those who are more talkative it sometimes helps to say, "Let's hear from those who haven't had a chance to say anything yet." Establish eye contact with quieter members and look less often at the "talkers." They will probably contribute regardless of your attention.

I was once at a committee meeting where the coordinator, Joanna, asked for a volunteer to greet people at an upcoming event. A few people responded with reasons why they couldn't do it. Marisue finally said, "I saw Joanna look at me when she asked, so I know she wants me to do it. Because I'm bringing others with me, though, I don't think I can." We all laughed as Joanna admitted that was what her eye contact had meant. Eye contact says, I'm listening or ready to listen to you.

5. *Keep sharing and answers on the point,* on the passage and in the present as much as possible. (See ground rules above.)

6. *Pace the questions* so that you finish in the time allotted. Note ahead of time questions you can omit if you are short of time. Keeping close track of time is important because you'll need time for the other components of group life, and people may have other time commitments afterward.

Summarizing Discussion
Summaries are needed periodically throughout the discussion. They review what has been said thus far. Often, when several have answered a question, a tangent catches attention and the main point becomes fuzzy or lost. Summarizing helps to recapture and tie together the main ideas and relate them to the passage being studied.

Summaries help as transitions too. "We have seen how Jesus served his disciples by washing their feet, and interacted with his disciples as he taught them. Now let's see how he prays for them."

Statements like these help us see threads which connect parts and keep us focused.

A final summary of what we have observed and interpreted can lead to application. This again brings into focus main themes, so that our application comes from what has been studied.

Until others take on functioning leadership roles, you can identify and encourage those you see who have this gift. "Chris, you usually listen to ideas well. Would you summarize what you've heard us say on this question?"

If you have committed yourselves to some kind of action as individuals or as a group, it is important that someone state what each person is to do, by when, and itemize any other details so that responsibility and expectations are well understood.

Finally, in an end summary it is often helpful if you can give a brief synopsis or introduction to the next week's study. This will help people want to return with some expectations. (An outline for preparing a Bible study is found among the Leadership Resources.)

Other Study Options
Most of your small group nurture time should be spent in Bible study. But your group can also use books, tapes, records, movies and so on. These can be interspersed with series of Bible studies for variety. A group may study the book of Jonah, discuss a tape at their next meeting, take a week for a social and then begin another Bible study series. (See the Nurture Resource section for ideas.)

Using these resources does not mean you do not need to prepare. Reading a booklet together can feed you all well. But discussion helps, and starting discussion with "Well, what did you think?" is not going to trigger much comment. As you did with Bible study, write out the major ideas the author (or speaker) is making. How do these fit together? What seems to be the one main idea communicated through it all? Then you need to prepare questions to stimulate discussion on the *main themes.*

1. Take each of the main ideas and ask how the speaker presented and supported these ideas. The most probable answers would be biblical texts, other writers, research, examples and illustrations. Have your group list them and tell how they supported an idea.

2. Note how these ideas are consistent with the whole gospel message. Which of the supporting ideas would you question, if any? Why?

3. Look for the thesis of this person's presentation. Was there a response for which he or she was looking? What was it? How do you want to respond to what you have heard?

4. Use more specific questions to get at particular thoughts you want discussed.

God has gifted many people with wisdom and an ability to communicate with us in speech, music or writing. Choose discriminately topics and materials appropriate for your group.

"They devoted themselves to the apostles' teaching and to the fellowship, to the breaking of bread and to prayer."

As you read this, you may say, "I understand the study as nurture, but aren't community and prayerful worship—the very ingredients you designate as 'other'—also nurture?" The answer is both yes and no. Yes, they are "other ingredients" of group life. But, no, they are not individual, distinct aspects of a group. We separate them for purposes of discussion, but they cannot be separated in our life. Even what we do as mission for others nurtures us, because we grow as we love more.

In small church groups people come together in dynamic interaction. We grow; we share; we respond in worship and obedience. It all works together as a lifestyle of believers who are being nurtured to follow Christ. To this lifestyle the early believers corporately devoted themselves.

Chapter 9
Worship

We worship God primarily because God is worth
receiving our praise and honor. Yet worship can also change our
lives.

Much of Christianity is punctuated with "oughts." We ought to
love one another, we ought to be a community, we ought to witness, we ought to obey God. But what motivates me to be obedient,
to witness, to be in community, is not a sense of "I ought" but
rather of "I want." When we are motivated from the heart rather
than from duty we are enthusiastic in our life and actions.

Reading the New Testament, I am amazed at how the life of the
church seems to be so much a natural result of their worship
experience. I see little exhortation to witness, witness, witness.
Rather the church grew and matured because of its worship experience with God.

In the early chapters of the book of Acts we see the experience of the resurrection bringing about worship and then enthusiasm to witness and live as Christians in the world. Realizing how great God is makes us *want* to witness and be obedient to his lordship. Jesus' disciples, awed by his resurrection, devoted themselves to prayer after he had ascended to the Father. With the Spirit's coming at Pentecost, this group of men and women burst into praise and witness. They were excited about what God had done in Christ. They were convinced their God was worthy to receive all praise and glory, and they eagerly proclaimed the news of the resurrection.

When my son's bike was stolen right from under him (we knew who had done it but were unable to prove it), the worship time of my small group meant a great deal to me. Focusing on God with others gave me perspective. I saw that, even though we live in a fallen world, the good news of knowing God was better than anything else life had to offer. Our group worship changed my whole attitude about that theft.

Worship can be a life changer. It can change the life of a group. Focusing on God, we become his people in the world. Effective small groups are like Moses and Israel in the wilderness. Moses said, "If thy presence will not go with me, do not carry us up from here" (Ex 33:15). He knew it was God's presence that made them unique (v. 16). Good groups will refuse to move forward one step without God.

How do groups sense and experience the presence of God? Worshiping together is one key way. It is a time for the small group to speak to itself of the great deeds of our God. Living in a world with so much turmoil, suffering and evil, we need to remind ourselves of who really is in charge of the universe. Thus worship refreshes and comforts us.

Worship—Honoring God

Although the group benefits from worship, our purpose is to honor our Lord and God. Christ is to be central in our lives as individuals, and he is to be central in our life as a group.

In John 4 Jesus speaks to a Samaritan woman about worship. She seems eager for an abstract talk about theology, but Jesus brings the discussion home. He emphasizes two things about worship.

First, God is looking for worshipers (Jn 4:23). He has taken the initiative. He is seeking us to worship him. He wants us to know him—and when we do, we worship him.

Second, God wants us to worship him in spirit and in truth. God is more concerned about our heart than any particular form of worship that we devise. Realizing this should encourage us in worship. He sees the spirit with which we approach him.

Worship Together

Small group leaders will want to keep worship relevant to the individuals and the group itself. One way is to keep worship integral with the other elements of small group life. For example, worship can introduce the nurture time; you can lead the group in a song that focuses on God and leads up to the study. Or, if the group has discovered something new about God, they can take a moment to respond in praise. Worship can also draw the group together as one in community before it sets off in some mission. We see the early church at prayer in Acts 4:24-31. After they prayed and worshiped the Lord, they moved out into the world with boldness. Worship can be the essence that bonds us and propels us to do the work of the kingdom.

God has created us to be creative ourselves, and our worship will reflect this creativity if we draw on the group's diversity. As a small group leader, you can help this creativity and diversity to flourish by encouraging it. You may need to offer suggestions, and you'll find several in the Worship Resources provided in chapter fifteen, pages 161-62. Small groups have written their own psalms, written new verses to favorite songs and hymns, and have even written their own lyrics and music to worship the Lord. Experiment!

Worship can, of course, be more than just singing hymns or praying. Some groups have even danced their worship. The criterion of "success" is whether the Lord is honored. Scripture tells us that Old and New Testament believers sometimes used their whole bodies to worship. They danced, lifted their hands, and fell on their knees and faces before God. Many of us are more hesitant to use our bodies. Leaders will need to be sensitive to all the group members in suggesting new forms of worship.

We all are used to specific ways of worshiping God which we have picked up from our varied backgrounds. If we don't hear and see what we're used to, we feel uncomfortable. Worse, we may think that another style is unspiritual. If Karen is used to raising her hands in worship and sees that Ruth doesn't do it, might it mean that Ruth doesn't feel the greatness of God as much as she does? To Ruth, Karen's hand raising may seem showy and dramatic rather than spiritual.

We make a grave mistake in judging someone else's worship through our own customs. As a group leader you can avert problems by bringing up the issue to discuss. Tell your preferences and learn theirs. Suggest that the group *experiment* periodically with a variety of worship styles that will stretch members to praise God more fully but not offend any participants. Variety in body posture, for example, can be a new and helpful experience to your group as you grow together. If there are some in your group with a particular style that they enjoy but which is unfamiliar to the others, allow them an occasion to lead in worship. With your initiative and sensitivity, members of the group can come to appreciate a variety of ways of worshiping that will draw you together in the Spirit of Christ.

Without worship our small groups will not realize the great power available to them in the presence of God. With God at the center of the group, vitality will extend throughout the world. In

Acts 17 we read that the early Christians turned the world upside down. May this be true of us as we worship our God in spirit and truth, as we offer our lives as living sacrifices, our spiritual worship.

Chapter 10

Community

I need people with whom I can feel close, with whom I can share, and I need this regularly. I can easily feel ho-hum about the Christian life. I need others to pick me up and push me on. I can't live Christianity in isolation. It is hard for me to be challenged in the routineness of Sunday worship, Sunday-school classes of fifty and potluck fellowships. I need others with whom to share personally. To struggle over issues and to be challenged to grow.

Being in an ongoing small group gives one sure reward—growing relationships. Experiencing ups and downs together, we can, over a period of time, build close relationships. As everyone in the group gets to know us, we have feedback from them. And through them we come to know ourselves. We learn how best to function in the church, on the job, with others. We learn what kinds of things we do best and which we don't do so well.

Life Together

How can our small groups develop such community?

Building community takes more than a shared faith and common beliefs, and it takes more than time spent car-pooling together, or even talking. Community, as we said in chapter three, is devotion to one another based on our joint experience of God at work in us. It is like an intact family who are committed to each other because of their common ties. Our tie comes from Christ's work of redemption for us.

Christ has forgiven us. We are new people. Our identity and our relationships are rooted in this. We are not perfect; we are not better than others. We simply have believed in Christ's forgiveness for us. As we see our selfishness, arrogance and capacity to hurt others, we continue to need and draw on this forgiveness. This good news affects our relationship not only with God but also with others. Because we belong to God's kingdom, we are free to risk ourselves in involvement with others. It may not be easy. We may even get hurt. Or we could let people down. But we can try again.

Because God has accepted me in Christ, I am free to accept others as his. This is not the acceptance that says, "You are one of us if you are always likable, valuable to us and don't rock the boat." It says rather, "I love you. You do some dumb things. I don't always approve of what you do. But I want to be involved with you. We are in this family together."

Jesus defined his family when he said, "Whoever does the will of God is my brother, and sister, and mother" (Mk 3:35). Family is more than being related. It means involvement. For Christians it is active involvement in the lives of one another *for the sake of God's kingdom.* Sometimes groups focus on building community in their groups—support groups, care groups, couples clubs and so on—and neglect doing the will of God. The group will never hold its balance this way. But at certain times in our lives we need groups that concentrate on community. Someone just widowed needs a support group, a community of believers beside her and upholding her in this transition. And, as we saw in chapter six, when a group first begins meeting, community building is a necessary focus. People need to know each other before committing themselves to a longer action plan. There are times, therefore, when community must be the main ingredient. But we must keep in mind that our purpose ultimately goes beyond mutual support.

Building Community

Going for pizza, bowling and drinking lots of coffee—we call this fellowship. Does this strengthen the common ties of our group?

Most groups see this as their main way for getting to know each other. The number of cups of coffee drunk, however, is not a sure index to how close and committed a group is.

How then can we build real community?

1. Get to know each other.

In a small group you will become *acquainted* as you come together for study, worship and outreach. But you may never know much about the people unless you go beyond the niceties like "The study was such a blessing to me." The level of beliefs, values, interests and feelings lies deeper.

First of all, schedule time in the group meeting for talking about yourselves. Sometimes you may decide to do this in the whole group. Other times you may divide into pairs. One way is to discuss *specific* application from your Bible study: What has this passage said to me? What am I going to do about it?

Structured experiences help you get to know each other in slightly deeper ways. You may want to begin your third or fourth meeting by saying, "Let's go around and have each person give a 'weather report' describing how you feel tonight." You can do this periodically to get a reading of how people feel. It may change the rest of the evening!

Another idea you may want to use over a period of weeks is the

"Faith Line" or "Life Line," a diagram showing how they have seen their faith progress over several years. Have one or two members take fifteen minutes during your meeting to share theirs. Or they could take their life, explaining high and low points and how their pilgrimage in life has been affected by these. (See Community Resources for more ideas.)

Structured experiences help you to know things about each other that may come up in ordinary discussion or at least speed up the process. Be sure to choose ideas which are appropriate to the stage or commitment level of the group (see chapter six).

Second, schedule time with members outside the group meeting. Get together for lunch or for an evening. You'll want to know each other one to one and not simply in the context of many people. The stronger the one-to-one relationships, the stronger your group. A team plays best when members can play well with *each* member on it.

You may decide to have a prayer partner, someone you meet with regularly for sharing and prayer. Dividing your group into prayer partners gives everyone a chance for time together one on one. You can rotate people either every couple of weeks or stay with one person for a few months and then rotate.

While most of your time will be spent in your regular meeting, at someone's house or at church, your group will be healthier if you do a variety of things together. Play volleyball. Paint a Sunday-school room at your church. You might even try a weekend retreat together. Community life will also be enhanced as you work out your group's mission. All of these ideas can help you know one another better and feel freer to discuss your ideas, feelings and interests in the group.

2. Accept and enjoy diversity.

It won't take you long to notice that everyone in your group is not like you. People not only look different; they think differently, and they experience and express their feelings in unique ways.

Some are strong in expressing ideas; others summarize group ideas well. Some have a knack for hospitality. Others lead good Bible study discussions. Some open up quickly. Others take a while to think over what they say before talking.

I work with Ron. A visionary idea-person, he has five new ideas a day. He wants us to try out each one—*now!* He'd move the office furniture around daily if it helped a new idea. I am an analyzer, perfectionist, detail person. I want to understand all the pros and cons of an idea, modify it as we get new data and know the outcome before we begin. I like to move furniture, but only if there's a reason and if we plan the move.

You may say, "How ideal! You must complement each other well." We do, but only after several years of conflict. We had to learn to accept the differences and see each other's strengths before we could work together smoothly. I appreciate Ron's creativeness. I need it. Ron has had to learn to work with my detailed appraisal of his ideas. It takes time.

Your group needs time to let the differences come out and to accept the diversity. We need not only appreciate the differences but to learn how to work with one another *with* those differences. Ephesians 4 tells us that the gifts of the Spirit are given to equip us all for ministry and building up the body of Christ. Just so, our temperaments, our cultures and so on can help equip us. I've often heard it said that "John's rough edges smoothed out after he married Mary." Small group interaction can do similar things for each of us if we are willing to do three things:

First, acknowledge each one in your group as God's creation, God's chosen *person* loved by him. You may think, "It's a good thing God loves her as his own child because I'll never feel that way." Not every person will have warm, loving feelings about every other person in the group. You need to begin by saying, "This person really thinks differently than I do. I have trouble communicating with someone who is so settled in his ways. But he is still a person created and loved by God, and together we are all his children."

Second, acknowledge the differences. We would prefer to dwell on our similarities when differences make us uncomfortable. But these differences profoundly affect our relationships. They exist and we need to admit it. Are some members of the group theoretical? Is it hard for them to relate Scripture to life? Are others very practical, having trouble interpreting facts before applying them to their own situation?

Third, acknowledge strengths. Oftentimes we get so bogged down in our negative reaction to someone that we miss the really helpful aspects of this person. What does Phyllis add to our group? How does she aid the group, individuals, our process, the study, our mission? If you have trouble doing this, let others in the group help you. Your whole group may want to do a "Strength Bombardment" (p. 171). Have one person at a time sit in the middle of the room and then bombard him or her with positive traits: "I like the way you bring us back on track when we wander." "I like your hospitality to new people and to all of us." This is not a way to play down rough spots or problems. It is simply to keep them in focus. We often find that what bothers us, others appreciate. As I struggled learning to work with Ron ("Why does he have to have so many ideas to try out?"), someone said to me, "I'll bet working with Ron is really fun. He's so creative."

God is working through each person, and he uses all of us in ways needed by our group. We appreciate the others more as we see that they have strengths needed by the group.

3. Care for individual needs.

Tony came into our group obviously more subdued than usual. I decided to do a "round," and Tony's weather showed cloudy. Carey asked him to tell what was behind it. We listened and prayed.

One way to build a sense of togetherness and closeness is by being sensitive to members' needs and joining together to meet these needs. At times people need emotional support—times of transition, new jobs, hard times, a fire in the home. Listening to and praying for Tony pulled us together and released him to emotionally join us for the rest of the evening.

Sometimes we can meet specific needs—meals at a time of birth or death, for example. We both are and must become the body of Christ for one another—fingers to cook, feet to run errands, shoulders to cry on, arms for support and caring, ears to listen, hearts to understand and love.

4. Open up lines of communication.

Oftentimes we come into our group simply needing a haven from the pressures of life: "I've had a horrible day. Can I just unload for a few minutes?" We can't change one another's day, but being willing to listen and pray may give that person the lift she needs to face more days.

Sharing what we are thinking and feeling can bind us together with a sense of having common experiences and feelings. It also gives people a broader view of us. I was amazed to discover that many people see me as outgoing. As a single person I have more time alone than many of my married friends, and I'm probably most withdrawn and introspective during those times. But others don't see me withdrawing. When I'm with friends, sharing some of my thoughts, fears, dreams and disappointments, I open myself up to them in new ways. They can only know of my introspective nature if I tell them.

It is dangerous to assume people know what we are thinking. It also may be dangerous to think we are hiding our feelings well.

I see Bob yawn for the third time and I think, "He is bored with the study I am leading." I feel anxious and hurt. I wish he wouldn't come if he doesn't want to be here. Bob is thinking, "This is great stuff! I wish I weren't so tired so I could absorb it better. Why does Judy look at me so sternly?" Open communication on either side would alleviate hard feelings—Bob's saying, "You know I really like this group, but I'm tired from a recent trip so I don't know how with-it I'll be . . . but I'll try," or Judy's saying, "Bob, I see you yawning a lot and I'm a little anxious, thinking you are bored with the study."

This kind of communication can be risky. I don't want to be seen as emotional or out of control. If we want to know one another better, however, we need to be willing to risk and push ahead in our level of communication.

5. Be clear about expectations.

Spelling out expectations for group members can help avoid conflict and frustration. When will we meet? Where? How often? What will we study? How much do I have to know about the Bible to be in a Bible study?

Spell out expectations at the beginning. This gives some concreteness to the exploration stage when members are asking, "What is this group about?" After several meetings you can begin to make decisions as a group. Group consensus about anything which affects all members is a better decision for the group than one which one person makes. Most expectations, even when agreed to in a group covenant (pp. 142-43), need review at least every three months.

Some expectations that contribute to balanced small group life are worth verbalizing periodically:

1. "We want everyone to take an active part in group activities and discussion. This may mean some need to assert themselves beyond what is comfortable. Others may need to hold back their contributions to let someone else talk."

2. "We want as many group members present as possible at each small group activity." (You may want to spell this out in a covenant by saying that we don't meet unless everyone can come.)

3. "We will follow the four-ingredient model of a small group, so we will have some form of mission for our group."

4. "We will begin and end the formal part of our meeting on

time, though we may agree to chat informally beyond the set time."

Working Through Problems

Difficult times come in even the best of groups. If we are truly devoted to one another and our group's purpose, we'll work through these tensions. Open communication and clear expectations are key.

Some problems occur frequently and are easy to spot. At the risk of appearing simplistic, I've charted these with their symptoms and some suggestions for handling them (see figure 9). Consider trying these steps before giving up or thinking you have a hopeless case on your hands. Above all, approach each situation in earnest prayer.

Talk to your small group coordinator or pastor about the problems of your group, especially if they persist. Either may give the help and encouragement you need.

The Lord has given us to one another for strengthening each other to corporately serve him more effectively. We do need each other!

Figure 9. Troubleshooting in small groups.

Symptom	Problem	Approaches
Members come late	Group pattern to start late. Exact time not clear.	Set definite time. Begin promptly. Discuss with group: "We're having trouble getting going. Is it too early? Are there conflicts?" Let members respond.
Agreed-on preparation not completed	Too much expected. Not clear how it relates to what group will do. Lack of commitment (may relate to being too busy and other priorities).	Be realistic. May need to change expectations. Check to make sure group understands and agrees to preparation.
Quiet members	Questions asked are too hard or too easy; not enough observation questions asked. Not prepared. Lack of openness. Leader and others not handling silence, jumping in too quickly.	Follow sequence of observation before interpretation. Have quiet member read passage out loud. Remind members: "Verbal people need to hold back at times; quiet members need to force themselves to speak up. Direct questions (not one no one else can answer) to quiet person. On an application question, do a round where each person in the circle responds. Allow time after question for people to think.
Overly talkative members	Outgoing. Doesn't like silence. Sees things quickly.	Talk to privately. Mention that we need silence after some questions to look and reflect. Ask help in drawing out others. (Suggest he ask, "What do some of the rest of you think?")
Issue causing disagreement	Verbal people "win out." Tangents. Not accepting differences.	State ground rules. Try to stick to passage or subject at hand. Suggest they discuss problem after the meeting. Agree that there are differences of opinion on this; on what can we agree?
Always-right members	Knows right way for everything. Knows only right interpretation of passage.	Avoid arguing right and wrong with person. Put focus back on passage, to collect more data and summarize. Let facts clarify. Help group look for alternatives and see "right" person's frame of reference. "In what circumstances might John's interpretation hold true?"

Symptom	Problem	Approaches
Disagreers	"But" is favorite word: "That's true, *but* . . ." May hold group back from action or conclusions, causing group to stagnate.	Give feedback to disagreer: "What exactly causes your hesitation?" Confront group with choice of holding back (no risk) or going ahead (with risk but also growth): "How can we get around this objection?"
Pacing slow or fast	Too much time on some parts. Little interaction. Questions too simplistic (or too general). Full answers not sought. Application too general.	Plan time for each component. Move parts along with good transitions. Test study questions with a coleader; are they clear, open but not overly general? Ask for specifics in sharing. Push for all of answer: "What else?"
Conversational prayer stifled	Lack of trust. New to members. Not aware of specifics for prayer.	Spend more time building community and praying for needs. Pray in direct and specific statements or requests. Discuss conversational prayer; pray on one topic before moving to another. Respond to study in prayer.
Group ingrown; no growth or mission	Purpose not clear. Study not motivating. Limited sense of growth of God's kingdom. Fear.	Plan nonthreatening activities to which you can invite others; have active outreach where new members are added to and cared for by small group. Center Bible study and worship on character of God, purposes of God, aspects of group life or life of the church.
Superficial sharing	Leader not setting example. Application not specific. Community building not challenging growth as a group.	Plan community exercises carefully for stage of development. Ask for specifics in sharing. Be open and specific in own sharing. Meet in one-to-ones outside group for sharing and prayer.
Members with ongoing problems	Problems dominate group life. Member monopolizes group with personal crises.	Talk individually to the person, suggesting resources for help (counseling). Help group see its purpose, identity. (Church groups are not therapy groups.) Continue in prayer and loving support.

Chapter 11

Mission

A small group from a local church goes caroling the day after Christmas. People ask, "Isn't Christmas over?" The group explains why they carol even after Christmas. They also distribute small gifts. Their witness sparks people's curiosity. During an age when Christmas has devolved to commercialism and sentimental tradition, the group provides a provocative alternative. Christ is lifted up.

Another church asks each small group to "adopt a missionary," thereby becoming the church's official liaison with that overseas ministry. Corresponding monthly, the group learns about the missionary's needs, assisting as possible and praying regularly. When the missionary returns on furlough, the small group acts as host and provides welcome hospitality.

Another small group has committed itself to working with a local hospice that gives relief and shelter to the needy. Group members pledge two hours a week to serve at the center. While the members don't always work simultaneously, their mutual involvement links them together.

These three small groups take seriously the fourth component of small group life—mission. Each group does it differently. They have different commitments, relationships, audiences, goals and activities. But each group has determined to make an impact for Christ's glory on the world. And each will be stronger because of this effort.

My favorite type of small group is one that forms around a particular mission opportunity. In other words, the "rallying cry" or "gathering note" is a common concern, whether prayer for missions in Latin America, hospitality to international students or an evangelistic heart for the neighborhood. Such groups know where they are heading. The community, nurture and worship of the group fuel the mission. These groups start off as launched rockets. They are dynamic, explosive forces used by God. Although the leader needs to make sure the "superactivists" in the group invest ample energy developing relationships, these groups are rarely grounded.

Groups can, of course, start with a concentration on some different component, such as a study of Romans. Or they may begin with an emphasis on community. Yet if groups intend to grow, they must develop a solid understanding of and involvement in some aspect of mission as well.

Highlights from Acts

In the book of Acts we see a marvelous sampling of Christian groups committed to reaching out beyond themselves toward their world. In some cases it's hard to determine whether these clusterings were small or large. Yet in them we find examples, inspiration and ideas for effective outreach. (The mission activity illustrated in each episode is italicized.)

Acts 1: Having been promised the power of the Holy Spirit and having been commanded to be Christ's witnesses locally and worldwide, the Twelve gathered with several women and Jesus' brothers to *pray.* Their prayers were answered. Fueled and filled by the Holy Spirit, they began to *preach,* igniting an enormous revival. Three thousand were added to their number.

Acts 4: Life in the early church matured: "Now the company of those who believed were of one heart and soul, and no one said that any of the things which he possessed was his own, but they had everything in common. And with great power the apostles *gave their testimony* to the resurrection of the Lord Jesus, and great grace was upon them all. There was not a needy person among them" (vv. 32-34). The group had developed an astonishing depth of community. They *supplied the material needs* of one another—undoubtedly assisting brand-new converts as well as veteran members. But the great benefits of their community were not kept quietly to themselves. Their verbal testimony was bold.

Acts 6: An unfortunate insensitivity by the majority, coupled with the overextension of a few key people, demanded some careful problem solving. The Twelve decided to create a small group of seven with a specific objective—to *serve* food at the tables and distribute it to the Hellenistic widows who had been previously neglected. The task was by nature mundane. But even simple tasks may help bring spiritual results, for we read that "the number of the disciples multiplied greatly in Jerusalem" (v. 7).

Acts 13: The Lord told the church at Antioch, a group of unknown size, to commission Barnabas and Paul to carry the gospel to the gentile world. Although it must have been tough to let these two pivotal members depart, the church complied. Barnabas and Paul left, strongly undergirded with fasting, prayer and blessing.

Acts 15: A theological debate threatened to divide the embryonic church. To regain peace and harmony, "the apostles and the elders were gathered together to consider this matter" (v. 6). The group listened to the two opposing perspectives and sought the Spirit's guidance. As a result, they discerned that God's salvation to the Gentiles was one of faith and grace, not one of cultural rules and physical regulations. The spiritual discernment of the group successfully unraveled a crucial truth from a cultural entanglement. Thus a *problem was solved.*

Acts 16—17: The apostle Paul's missionary tours were not a one-man show. Rather, Paul gathered around him a team that included at least Silas, Timothy and Luke (Acts 17:4, 14, 34; 16:16 says "we," apparently including the author Luke in the band). Paul's *ministry and outreach* were, in actuality, accomplished by a small group, working together as a company of God's ambassadors. As the disciples' gifts and talents were *coordinated,* new strength and resources were pumped into the emerging church.

Acts 24: In addition to proclaiming the gospel, Paul's team urged the scattered Christian churches to financially assist the troubled church in Jerusalem. The Bible does not tell us exactly what the problem was; but Paul's small group took seriously its responsibility to help.

The Basic Elements of Small Group Mission

Mission is sharing in word and deed the good news of Christ's love to people in need. Christians, individually and together, must reach beyond themselves. As God's "divine power has granted to us all things that pertain to life and godliness" (2 Pet 1:3), we are responsible to apply his power and love to change individuals and society. But how, why and to whom?

What kind of outreach? Mission encompasses the broadest concept of sharing God's love in word and deed. It's more than simply supplying food to the hungry. It's more than simply proclaiming the human need to repent and believe. Outreach includes evangelism *and* social action, local concern *and* worldwide concern, efforts within our culture *and* efforts cross-culturally, help that is spiritual *and* help that is material. The outreach component of a small group might mean anything from raising financial and prayer support for a new missionary heading for Morocco to caring for an unwed mother and her child. The biblical mandate includes both doing "the work of an evangelist" (2 Tim 4:5) and loving "in deed and in truth" (1 Jn 3:18). Look at your group's mission and check to see if it is *both/and* in outreach.

Why reach out? The goal of mission is to help people physically, emotionally, spiritually and/or socially. The task starts where the group is and expands to the ends of the earth. Humanly speaking, the challenge far exceeds our imagination and resources. If we only concentrated on our limitations, we would quickly quit in despair. We'd be like the disciples who, having counted five loaves and two fishes, found the proposal to feed five thousand preposterous. Yet, as the Twelve discovered, the crucial factor was the presence of Christ. For us the promise remains—"Lo, I am with you always . . ." We seek mission because of God's compassion and because of his commission. We go into mission by his guidance and with his presence.

Three primary reasons motivate us to share Christ. First, God has commanded that we "go . . . and make disciples of all nations" (Mt 28:19). Paul affirms this, saying, "Him [Christ] we proclaim, warning every man and teaching every man in all wisdom, that we may present every man mature in Christ" (Col 1:28). If we are to be God's disciples, we must obey Jesus' command.

Second, those in need require our compassionate assistance. Jesus set the model, exercising deep concern for those around him. Not out of condescension but out of deep care, he referred to them as "lost," "sick," "hungry" and "poor." Sometimes he meant they were literally sick and poor. Other times Jesus meant the terms in a figurative, spiritual way. People then and now have a desperate need to know God.

Third, our involvement in outreach increases our faith and our own experience of Christ's love and power. The disciples must have marveled, despite their embarrassment, as they collected twelve baskets of leftover bread and fish. They were learning about their Lord's sufficiency. As we step forward in faith, as we exceed our personal expectations and strengths, as we overcome our fears and take risks, we receive first-rate opportunities to observe our God's power and presence.

There is one further benefit gained when small group members involve themselves in outreach: they bond together more quickly and more strongly. The gifts of different members are identified, utilized and coordinated. Service, evangelism, faith, acts of mercy and liberal contribution may be especially valuable gifts. When the complementary qualities of the group mesh together, the group gathers great strength. We lose something important if mission is simply a private, personal activity.

Reach out to whom? This is a tough question. It's like asking, "Who is my neighbor?" The answer opens up a world of possibilities—a person, a tribe, a nation or a continent. Neighbors may be fifteen yards or fifteen thousand miles away. They may be in your church or in another congregation. They may be people who have never heard the name of Christ.

Small groups often reach out on several levels simultaneously. A group may want to be involved locally, such as with a refugee family or a neighborhood evangelistic Bible study, and may want also to be praying for and corresponding with a missionary family in Hong Kong. Decisions need to be made with the consensus of the whole small group so that they have a focus.

As for the question "Who are those in *need?*" the answer is equally broad in scope. Spiritual, material and social needs abound. You may want to begin by praying for the greatest needs that are closest. As the group gains momentum, it can adjust its sights.

Reach out when? In the early stages of group development,

while the members are getting acquainted and organized, mission may consist mostly of supporting what participants are already doing outside of the group. It might be praying for friends or for various nations around the world. Eventually, however, the time will come for a more corporate approach. Gather and evaluate your thoughts as a group, and then make your decision for a specific project.

Groups occasionally fail to develop a group mission for a variety of reasons. Maybe the leader is hesitant at first to mention outreach. This is unfortunate because the initial meeting is crucial in setting people's expectations. If members can see from the start that mission is part of their reason for existence, they will be less inclined to balk when, later on, outreach events require more of them. Or perhaps mission remains on hold because the leader is waiting until everyone in the group "has his act together." Don't wait. After three or four meetings, move the group toward reaching out. It will stimulate growth in the members.

Building Mission into the Life of a Small Group

How can you move your group toward outreach? The following ideas are not formulas, but they may help get you going.

1. Remind members that the four components are interrelated and that they work together to strengthen a small group. For example, if a group is studying Acts 4, they could pray to become more bold evangelistically. The Bible study gives spiritual *nurture* which energizes the mission. Seeing how God has worked through his people in the past heightens too the group's *worship*. As members share their fears about witnessing or encountering opposition, they gain a sense of *community*. As a group they can then begin with a *mission* to share Christ with specific friends—a neighbor, a colleague at work, a tennis partner or someone in their carpool. A little later they may want to have a more corporate outreach to these people through literature distribution, an investigative

Bible study or perhaps a party during which someone briefly explains his or her relationship with Christ.

2. Discuss how the good news of Jesus Christ is indeed news that is good to modern people. Analyze 1 Peter 2:9: "that you may declare the wonderful deeds of him who called you out of darkness into his marvelous light." What are Christ's deeds? Why are they wonderful? What kind of darkness previously surrounded you? What is your present experience of God's light? Such a discussion helps members grapple with the specifics of God's love, and helps them personalize and communicate it.

3. Set the perspective from the beginning that outreach is natural and necessary. Involve the group initially in nonthreatening forms of outreach, projects in which they feel confident. Workdays in a food distribution center might be a good beginning effort. As consensus and mission-consciousness increase, help the group plow into more stretching forms of mission, such as sacrificial giving or a Christian booktable at a shopping mall on Saturday.

4. Help the group develop the necessary skills for effective outreach in whatever area they have chosen. In many cases this will mean helping members master a verbal presentation of the gospel. Provide them with a basic outline. Try some role playing. As people feel better equipped, their outreach will flow more naturally.

5. Press for consensus and group ownership. As the writer of Hebrews exhorts, "Let us consider how to stir up *one another* to love and good works" (10:24). The group becomes a think tank and offers mutual accountability. Each group needs to reach consensus on what specific task God has for them. Group ownership will enable everyone to work as a team in a much more thoroughgoing and wholehearted way. You'll need the assurance that God has led you into this mission when frustration, setbacks and opposition hit.

6. Plan time for planning. To reduce undesirable last-minute panic, begin the planning process far enough in advance. Some

informal mission events can be adequately planned in a week. Major outreach events, like hosting a citywide preaching mission, obviously take a year or more.

7. Keep in mind that a small group does not *always* need to be immersed in outreach. It may choose to do something weekly, or it may decide on semiannual events. At times another component may take precedence.

8. Surround all outreach in prayer. As we ask God to intervene in lives and events, we learn to rely on his strength rather than ours. While God commands us to be stewards of our gifts, energy and resources, it is not our job to convert people. The Holy Spirit does that. Our role is to serve as signposts pointing to Christ. Prayer reminds that we aren't the prime movers in building the kingdom of God.

Obstacles to Outreach

Virtually every suggestion above has an inverted form that can keep a group out of active mission. Let's look at these and see what we can do about such obstacles.

1. The group wrongly assumes that any of the four group components, including mission, is optional. If a group never engages in serving others, it becomes self-serving, lazy, ingrown. Counter the problem by returning to the biblical model of the four components.

2. Members feel that the good news is not wanted. Because our society sees values and truth as relative, it's hard for Christians to get excited about spreading the gospel. But according to Scripture outreach is not optional.

3. Overly ambitious programs can demoralize a group. Mission efforts should stretch members, not cause them to snap. Look for practical, achievable activities as you start out.

4. Outreach may fail because members are unequipped for their roles. Prepare them ahead. If training is needed, provide it. (See

Mission Resources.)

5. If even one person is unconvinced, there can be trouble. Active dissent or disagreement means that you haven't got consensus. Back to the drawing board!

6. Rushed or panicky efforts can be very dissatisfying. Allow adequate time to plan. Good planning can take much longer than you might imagine. Occasionally, you may want to substitute some planning for the nurture time. Or the group may agree to a special meeting precisely ior planning.

7. Enthusiastic outreach can lessen sensitivity to particular members' needs. Don't ignore someone's views because the majority of people are caught up in activity. You may need to call timeout to tend to someone who feels left out, whose feelings have been hurt or who has other needs.

8. Projects done without prayer will generate nothing but wasted energy. As Jesus told his disciples, "Apart from me you can do nothing" (Jn 15:5). So pray!

Two other common obstacles frequently surface when a group is especially geared toward evangelism. First, one member may prove resistant or stubborn, unwilling to participate in the evangelistic effort all the rest agree on. Discuss the problem individually with the person, explaining Romans 1:16. You may want to clarify with him or her the group's vision. Perhaps ask why this person wants to be part of the group. Ultimately the person may need to find another group, one that has a mission emphasis more compatible to him.

A second problem occurs when you've got non-Christians regularly participating in your small group, and you want now to do an evangelistic outreach. It's fine if they can participate on a level where they feel comfortable. Maybe they can pitch in with logistics such as setting up chairs or bringing desserts. If not, perhaps they will quietly observe. They may learn a lot about the love of Christ and your love for people as the project proceeds. But don't let fear of offending them paralyze your group into inactivity.

Steps in Planning

How does a group begin to get into mission? Let us suggest a process your group can follow.

1. Reaffirm your commitment that mission be a basic component of the group's life and purpose. Pray together for God's leading.

2. Take time as a group to dream out loud. List all the possible ideas for outreach that members can imagine collaborating on. Estimate for each the time commitment necessary.

3. Have all members spend a few minutes listing their own interests and identifying one or two gifts they think other members have. All should assess the amount of time they are willing to invest. Take turns sharing insights.

4. Using these insights about gifts and interests, discuss which ideas now seem most appropriate. The leader may help the group narrow the choice to three or four possibilities.

5. Discuss the pros and cons of each of these three or four ideas, searching for a consensus to emerge as to which is most suitable. Once one is chosen, the leader should reaffirm that everyone is agreed.

6. If consensus cannot be reached, stop to pray together. Think and pray about it individually until the next group meeting, but agree to decide finally at that time.

7. Determine what must be done, when it should be done and by whom. Then, bathing the concern in prayer, work to make it happen!

As outreach was central to the life and ministry of Jesus, so too it must be basic to the life of a Christian small group. Although it will demand much of the group's time, energy, money and spiritual gifts, the results can be enormously satisfying. Mission may well generate your small group's finest memories.

Part 3
The Broader Vision

Chapter 12

A Strategy for Small Groups in Your Church

Christian leaders often dream of multiplying the ministry of their church one hundredfold. Small groups have provided the answer in numerous churches. They have become the launching pad for regular exercise of spiritual gifts both within the Christian community and outside to a world captive in sin.

Imagine a city saturated with more than ten thousand small groups that serve as evangelistic teams pressing the gospel into every section of the city: neighborhoods, offices, factories, schools, hospitals, government agencies—everywhere! Some churches have made this dream a reality. A church of more than 100,000 members in Seoul, Korea, includes almost everyone in a small group. In fact, it is through the small groups that the church has grown so rapidly, both in numbers of new people and in their spiritual growth.

Consider this strategy for church growth: If a church has most of its members in small groups of six people each, and if each small group adds just one new person each year, *the size of the church would double in five years*. Surely it is a realistic goal for each small group to find just one new person each year to bring into the fold.

The Church Body Functioning as a Body

Imagine the potential for pastoral care if all the members of a congregation were in caring small groups. Psychologists have discovered that many clients improve more rapidly in small group therapy than through individual counseling. The potential for body-life nurture and healing in small groups is great. Through a complete network of small groups involving all the church, a call could go out to the small group leaders whenever an emergency arises. The group members could assist the pastor in situations like the death of a family member, a financial crisis and so on. They could visit group members in the hospital, bring in meals for the sick, loan cars, help with child care and pray specific prayers.

I first began to distinguish between the church *as a building* and the church *as a body of believers* when I was in high school. My family had joined a church which was just starting. For several years we met in a local elementary school, which hardly fit my image of a church! It was the people and what we did in the school gymnasium that transformed the building into a place of worship. The people were the church.

Church structures, whether physical or organizational, must be designed to fit the purpose of the church. This is as true for church boards and small groups as for buildings. If we're going to make small groups the basic building blocks of the church, then we need to look carefully at the overall design for the whole body. Small groups and large groups must complement and support each other.

Don't Rush!

Some organizations have rushed into a small group program to keep up with the trend without considering how the small groups should fit in with such in-place programs as Sunday-school classes and midweek prayer meetings. Or groups are started without carefully planning how to train and nurture the small group leaders on a continuing basis. These groups are heading for trouble.

How then do we design a structure that is effective and lasting? First of all, recognize that you can choose your structure only after the church has agreed on its purpose and strategy (see figure 10).

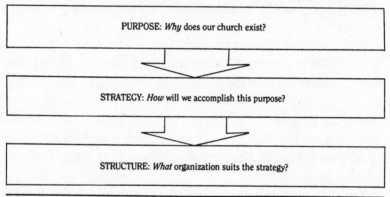

Figure 10. Purpose, strategy and structure.

Start with a clear understanding of the purpose of your church. The purpose determines the strategy, and the strategy determines the structures. Too often we have turned things around. We may have inherited structures, so we try to design a program that fits into them without asking *why* we need to do it. It may be time to turn such thinking upside down. What is our real purpose? What do we want to achieve?

For as long as I can remember, our church had Sunday school at 9:30 A.M. and its worship service at 11:00 A.M. But we had a problem: only half as many people came to Sunday school as to worship. Since our church strongly wanted to train people in the Scripture, to build them up and equip them for service, we felt that Sunday school played an important role. So we began to look at our *strategy*. We asked ourselves, "How can we get more people into these Sunday-school classes? How can we make better use of the good structure we already have?"

Someone suggested a new approach, that we have worship from 9:30 to 10:30, followed by twenty minutes of coffee and rolls, and then Sunday school at 11:00. Most of our people would make the extra effort to arrive an hour and a half earlier because they were committed to worship. Once there, they were likely to stay. It worked! Immediately Sunday school was attended nearly as well as worship.

With the right *strategy* we could turn the *structures* around to better fulfill our *purpose*. Structure serves strategy, just as "the sabbath was made for man, not man for the sabbath" (Mk 2:27).

Clarify the Purpose

How clear are you about the purpose of your church? A statement of purpose is crucial. Members should be able to recite it almost without thinking.

The statement of purpose tells why the church exists. For example, a church may decide its purpose is to be the body of Christ which equips members for ministry both within and beyond its community. Or it may set as its purpose that all members develop three key relationships—toward God in *worship*, toward fellow Christians to help them in *spiritual maturity* and toward the world to be *redemptive*. Try to write a one-sentence statement of your church's purpose: "Our purpose is . . . "

Develop a Strategy

Once you have a clear statement of purpose, take a hard look at the main strategies you are using. Are they moving you toward your goal? If part of your purpose is to help the members grow into the likeness of Christ, what is your church doing to make it happen? Does the Christian education committee have a strategy—or merely a set of old programs they feel they must keep going?[1]

If our church's purpose is to help people grow in their prayer life and to encourage group prayer, it may be that replacing the mid-week prayer service at the church with a number of small groups meeting in homes will actually increase the number of people praying and the quality of their prayer life. Many churches have adopted this strategy. As new people come into the church, they are encouraged to join a small group where they can build some close friendships, grow as disciples and receive training for outreach.

For this system to work, however, other supporting strategies need to be in place. For example, there must be a plan for feeding new people into small groups. Here's how one church does it:

1. As people come to the worship service at church, they sign a visitor's card in the pew.

2. The cards are given to the church secretary, who sends a welcome letter which includes a folder and other information on small groups.

3. The cards go to a visitation committee.

4. People from the committee visit newcomers within two weeks. They establish rapport, tell more about the church, answer questions and invite them to join a small group (telling them where, when and so on).

5. After the visit, the person from the visitation committee calls a small group leader to tell about the newcomer and to encourage the small group leader to make contact.

6. A follow-up letter goes to the new person a week later.

Look again at the purpose statement you just wrote (p. 124). Now try to formulate a statement of your church's strategy: "Our primary strategy for bringing about our purpose is . . . "

Put the Structure in Place

Once a clear strategy is worked out, you are ready to set up your structures. Howard Snyder writes, "The small group can become the basic structure in a local church if there is the vision for it and the will to innovate. The change cannot come, however, without rethinking traditional programs and structures. The midweek prayer meeting may have to go in favor of a number of midweek small group meetings so the small groups do not take up another precious weeknight or become something merely tacked on."[2]

Small groups need to be part of a network that ties all the church structure together. Elmbrook Church, near Milwaukee, Wisconsin, designed a small group program to serve its three thousand members. They have three types of small groups: (1) peer groups (children, youth, college age), (2) interest groups (singles, women, men, missions, choir), and (3) geographic groups (neighborhoods). All the groups function under the responsibility of a small group pastor (see figure 11).

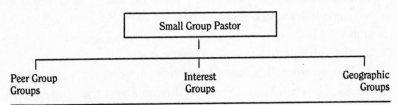

Figure 11. Example of a small group structure.

The neighborhood groups, which are organized within specific geographic locations, each have ten to twelve participants. Newcomers are fed into groups through a visitation program. For every six groups in a particular geographic section of the city there is a regional coordinator. These regional coordinators are then under the care of a pastoral coordinator (see figure 12), who is the person in touch with the small group pastor. And so it is with each of the group types.

To keep this structure working effectively requires regular training, motivation and information. Elmbrook publishes a monthly

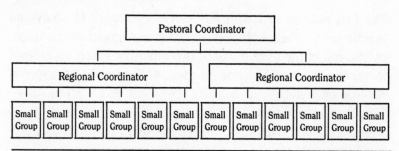

Figure 12. Neighborhood groups with leaders.

newsletter which is sent to their small group leaders, to help train them and to give them ideas for leading, and regional coordinators meet with them quarterly. The church also offers a course each quarter for *new* neighborhood group leaders, and each year the pastoral staff trains new regional coordinators through a twelve-week course. And once a year brush-up seminars for leaders old and new review the basic strategy of the small group program and introduce new resources.

The Elmbrook model has demonstrated how a variety of programs and structures can work together to support the small group strategy.

Starting from Ground Zero

A complex program like the one at Elmbrook does not just spring out of the ground overnight. Blair Anderson, pastor of an average-sized church, wanted to develop a strategy that would accomplish four important goals in his church: (1) expand the ministry of adult Christian *education,* (2) build greater *community* among the members, (3) provide for more care and *nurture* of the members, and (4) develop a means of increasing *ministry* to others, both within and without the church. He was willing to start small, move slowly and build steadily over a number of years. He knew that quality takes time to develop.

Blair began the project with one very influential lay leader, Ray.

The first year he met with Ray every other week to study and brainstorm for the eventual small group ministry of their church. By the end of the second month two other lay leaders had joined them, Ann Marie and Joanne. The four of them attended a special seminar on small group ministry sponsored by Churches Alive.[3] Here they learned some basic principles, saw a model small group structure and received some written resources to use as they prepared their strategy.

For the next six months the four of them met to study the resources in more detail and to design a plan for the next five years. Because they wanted their small group program to be an *official* part of the overall church ministry, fitting in with the total task of Christian education in the church, they wrote and submitted a proposal for groups to the adult Christian education committee for approval. The church board of administration also approved the proposal.

Next, the task force of four looked through the entire church directory (fifteen hundred people) and identified about sixty-five members who had the potential to be good small group leaders and who were available for such a ministry. All sixty-five were sent written invitations to a weekend (Friday night and Saturday) informational meeting. Phone calls or personal visits followed up the letters.

Thirty of the sixty-five came to the Small Group Information Clinic and learned about the overall vision for small groups in the church, the five-year plan for building toward it, how they might be part of the process, and the four purposes of each proposed small group—Bible study, sharing, prayer and outreach. At the end of the clinic they were challenged to prayerfully consider if they should be in this program; they were to respond within two weeks. About twenty of the thirty agreed to be involved.

Two training groups were started, each with ten potential leaders and two members of the original task force. These groups met weekly for the next two years. Their meetings ran two hours, or longer. The weekly commitment helped them develop strong community, build deep trust and get into a regular pattern of meeting.

Each week the facilitator filled out an evaluation form on the progress of the group and members (see under Leadership Resources). The small group facilitators met briefly each Sunday morning to review the evaluation forms, reflect together, pray and coordinate future activities.

After about a year and a half, several key individuals from each group were selected to spin off and lead new groups, a process which would train an additional twenty new potential small group leaders. The task force had individual interviews with each of the potential new small group participants to assist them in understanding the purpose of the small groups, the commitment needed, assignments and so on. At the same time, the task force implemented Discovery Classes. These classes met during the Sunday-school hour at the church for seven weeks. They reviewed for new and not-so-new Christians some basics of the Christian life: assurance of salvation, prayer, victory over temptation, forgiveness of sin, guidance for daily living and ways of witnessing. By the third year of the program two more small groups were functioning and the original task force were taking advanced training. Figure 13 gives an overview of the church's five-year plan.

Principles to Grow By

The process this church followed illustrates several important principles for developing any small group program.

Research and plan carefully. The team took most of the first year just to gather information, review programs from other churches and plan carefully for themselves. They planned five years of development.

Build quality patiently. The church did not rush into a small group program just to keep up with the trend. They resisted the

Year	Activity (goals)
1	Research and plan
2	Identify potential small group leaders; hold information clinic; set up two training groups
3	Start two additional groups; get further training for task force
4	Dissolve training groups and start five long-term groups
5	Add additional groups as people are ready

Figure 13. A five-year plan for small groups.

temptation to appoint dozens of untrained leaders immediately and assign all the members to a group. Rather, they started small, moved slowly and built steadily.

Train leaders well. Training was a strong focus in the entire program. All the leaders were in good small groups for over a year before they branched out to lead their own groups. They saw leadership modeled before having to do it.

Establish a review system. Small group leaders evaluated their meetings and met together regularly to establish quality control. They revised methods and goals as they worked through difficulties and grew.

Coordinate with other church programs. Small groups were officially part of the adult Christian education program. They related to the Sunday morning program, with classes sometimes training leaders, sometimes preparing members for participation.

A small group is not an isolated cell in the body of Christ. It must be supported by a network of relationships with other groups in the church. All groups, large and small, express the organic unity of the church. Together they provide the means for us "to grow up in every way into him who is the head, into Christ" (Eph 4:15).

Part 4
Compendium of Resources

Chapter 13

Leadership Resources

The materials in this chapter are arranged to follow an order in which a leader might likely need them. They move from job description (who leaders are and what their responsibilities are) to tools that will help leaders lead well. Included are some actual forms for members and leaders to fill out at various stages, especially to help evaluate what's happening in your times together.

Probably of most help are the sections on how to lead a group meeting, how to lead a Bible study and how to make a group covenant. The last section of the chapter will help you and your church train others for leadership and design a total-church small group program.

Job Description: Small Group Leader
■ The primary job of the small group leader is to model Christian discipleship. The following qualifications are important:
☐ A regular devotional and prayer life
☐ Good family relations
☐ Good physical and emotional health
☐ Involvement in the local church
☐ A commitment to the mission of the church
☐ A regular financial contributor to the work of God

■ The small group leader plans and conducts small groups, seeing to it that each meeting includes all four elements.
☐ Nurture: Being fed by God to grow into the likeness of Christ through Bible study, Christian literature, tapes, sharing
☐ Worship: Praising and magnifying God by focusing on his nature, actions and words; prayer, singing, praises, readings, creative expression
☐ Community: Fellowship centered around shared Christian experiences; sharing needs (spiritual and physical), having fun, developing spiritual gifts, encouraging prayer partnerships, interceding
☐ Mission: Reaching out in Christ's love to people in need; helping the group focus on the need for a mission from the start facilitating training of small group members in evangelism; helping the group define its mission and plan a strategy for accomplishing it

■ The small group leader helps members make a covenant together about commitments to one another (pp. 142-43).

■ The small group leader is a shepherd for the group members.
☐ Meets with members on an individual basis to encourage their spiritual growth and their involvement in leadership training and other church events
☐ Disciples one or two members to become coleaders and to assume responsibilities
☐ Encourages regular church attendance by each member
☐ Regularly prays for group members

■ A small group leader submits reports as needed and informs the small group coordinator or pastor of specific needs of small group members. He or she is willing to be trained further:
☐ Meeting with small group coordinator or pastor, as needed
☐ Attending regular training sessions as provided
☐ Studying recommended materials

Developing and Communicating Vision
Vision: Sight, ability to see what needs exist and what can be accomplished to meet these needs.

■ What is your vision for small groups in your church?

■ What is your vision for your small group?
□ Study the Scripture to see how God has worked and used his people to accomplish his purposes. The more familiar we are with God's purposes, the more his vision can develop in us. We depend on him to nurture that vision in us and bring it into reality.
□ Evaluate what needs exist in your church and community. How can a small group help meet those needs?
□ Be creative. Don't be limited by the past. What new things can be done by a group?
□ Ask God to give you wisdom.
□ Ask others for their ideas. Look to the visionaries. Share with others as your vision develops. Get their guidance and prayer.

■ How can you pass this vision on to others?
□ Write out your ideas so that you can communicate them clearly to others.
□ Speak to several people. Don't unload, but share a little at a time so that they can catch and digest what you are saying.
□ Begin to take steps toward your vision. Others want to join someone who is going somewhere, not just dreaming.
□ Follow up on those who seem genuinely interested. Spend time with them.
□ Pray that members of your group will grow in vision and in commitment to carry it out.

Personal Data Card

Having information on each of your members gives you contact information, ability to match up members by interests, an emergency contact if no one is home, ideas for outings or recreational activities in which your group can participate, areas in which the members can contribute their talents to the church. Have each member fill out a card with the following information:

Name _____

Address _____

_____

_____

Phone (home) _____ (business) _____

Next of kin (not in house) _____

Birthday _____

Hobbies _____

_____

Other areas of interest _____

_____

_____

_____

Physical activities enjoyed _____

_____

_____

_____

Small Group Meeting Planning Worksheet
Fill out prior to each meeting.

Date: _____

Time: _____

Purposes:

☐ To further nurture (_____ minutes):
(Include: The aim of my Bible study is to cause members to . . .)

☐ For worship (_____ minutes):

☐ To build community (_____ minutes):

☐ For mission (_____ minutes):

Preparing for and Leading a Small Group Meeting
■ Group vision
☐ Describe what you want your group to be like. (Be realistic!)
☐ Explain what you want your group to accomplish in your church, in their neighborhoods.
☐ Motivate your group to reach goals.
   1. Others will be motivated as you share your personal vision with them. Developing vision and committing oneself to it is often a gradual process.
   2. Encourage the four components in your group.
   3. Call people to commitment.

■ Group activities
☐ Meet weekly.
   1. Your nurture period should set the theme for each meeting. Try to pick activities for the three other components which come out of your time of nurture.
   2. Try new ideas. Tradition is not always best.
   3. Use experiences which are appropriate for the stage of group development.
   4. Time each activity so that your meetings begin and end on time.
☐ Spend time during the week with individuals.
☐ Spend time during some weeks doing group activities (meals and the like).

■ Group process
☐ Set the tone.
   1. Be early to the meeting. This sets a good example for others to follow and shows your commitment and delight in the group.
   2. Greet each member by name. Vary comments, but let each know he or she is welcome.
   3. Discern and deal with any immediate concerns on people's minds. Set a time for later discussion with those involved if a matter only involves one or two others.
   4. A leader models or sets the tone for the sharing that will go on. Your level of risk, trust, caring and sharing will be what other members will see as the "norm" for this group.
☐ Facilitate discussion.
   1. A circle without barriers is best for group discussion. If any come in late, make sure they are brought into the circle.
   2. Ask questions; don't lecture.
   3. Let people think after you have asked a question or asked for sharing. Relax. Don't fear silence.
   4. Never answer your own questions. Reword a question if the meaning is not clear.

5. Don't stop with one person's answering or sharing. Ask, "What else do you see?" or "What other ways are there?" or "Does anyone else have a different perspective?"

6. Don't struggle to get exactly what you think is the right answer. Better to let a few questionable responses go by than to discourage people from talking. However, if it is a matter of basic truth or the answer is wide of your aim, say something like "That's an interesting point of view. Does anyone else have a thought about this?" Avoid leaving an impression of confusion. Rather, sum up briefly, "I appreciate your sharing. I guess my thoughts are . . . because . . ."

7. Acknowledge each person's answer. Let each one know (verbally and nonverbally) that you are listening and that you appreciate the contribution. If it will help, ask clarifying questions: "Could you explain more?" Be natural in responding. If the idea is something new, simply say, "I hadn't seen that before. Thanks for pointing it out."

8. Try to have all included in group discussion. At times you may want to call on people. Don't give someone on whom you're calling the question no one can answer. Make them obvious or easily answered questions.

9. If someone talks too much, a helpful comment is "Let's hear from someone who hasn't had a chance to comment yet." Strive for balanced participation.

10. Keep sharing current and personal.

☐ Avoid quoting other sources, speakers, preachers, commentaries, books or experiences that are months or years removed from the group meeting.

☐ Encourage people to share things God has done in their lives this week or during the meeting.

☐ Keep sharing appropriate; too much personal sharing too close to a group's beginning can seem out of place and threatening.

☐ Facilitate involvement and commitment.

1. Delegate responsibilities, using people's talents and gifts.

2. As the group develops, decide on some goals together and commit yourselves to one another's and the group's growth (covenant).

3. Meet often with others outside of group meeting—prayer partners, meals together and so on.

4. Give opportunity for members to succeed. Encourage them if they fail.

Preparing and Leading a Bible Study

■ Before you begin, *remember* . . .

☐ It takes time—a minimum of two hours' preparation a week if you use a Bible study guide for nurture, a minimum of six hours if you are writing your own study.

☐ It is the Holy Spirit that will speak to people through the Bible. He is at work in you, in others and among you all as you study together.

■ Preparing a group Bible study

☐ Read through the entire book you will be studying. Observe main themes, repeated words, main characters, principal divisions.

☐ Look up historical background on the book. (Some of this can be picked up by reading the book itself.)

☐ Study each specific passage thoroughly on your own, even if you are using a guide.

    1. Make observations on each paragraph.

    2. Title paragraphs.

    3. Ask what is significant about what you have observed. What does it mean?

    4. How does each paragraph fit into the theme?

    5. Write down what you think is the main theme of the passage.

    6. Ask what meaning this passage has for you. What is God asking you to do to practice the truth of this passage (believe, repent, obey)? Study the passage until it grabs you personally. If the leader has met God through the Scriptures, excitement about the passage will come through to others, too. (See chapters eight and fifteen for further help.)

    7. Work through the study guide, answering every question.

☐ Prepare your goals and questions.

    1. Write out the purpose for your study based on the main idea in the passage. What meaning does that central truth have for each person in your group? The same central truth can have many applications. Therefore, application varies from person to person and group to group. Does this application have application for your group life together?

    2. Write (or choose from your guide) questions for your group study.

    ☐ Concentrate on those questions which center on the main purpose of the study.

    ☐ Throughout the study questions ask which cover observation, interpretation and application. Don't leave all the application until the end, in case you run short of time.

    ☐ Check questions out for clarity and brevity. Do they cover the material and move the group smoothly through the passage? Does one question lead to the next? Are you comfortable with the wording? If not, reword the question, keeping the content the same.

    ☐ Mark key questions that you won't want to miss if you run short on time.

3. Develop an introduction which excites the members about the study.
☐ Use needed background information.
☐ Review past studies if they lead into ideas for this study.
☐ Build curiosity.
☐ Don't give away the central truth, but help focus their thoughts on the content.
☐ Establish a point of identification between the group and the passage. Help people to get personally into the scene: "What do you feel, see, smell, hear?"
4. Pray for yourself and your group throughout this preparation.

■ Leading the Bible study
☐ Lead the group to discoveries through good questions. Christ often used a discovery method of teaching (Lk 7:40-43; 10:25-37).
☐ Be sure not to ruin the joy for others by simply telling them what you have found.
☐ State the ground rules at the first meetings and review them periodically. They are the following:
1. Approach the Bible fresh, open to learning as you would study a good textbook.
2. Avoid leaning on information from outside sources; let the text speak for itself.
3. Expect the text, not the leader, to answer questions.
4. Stay in the passage under consideration, and stay on the point under discussion.
☐ Pace the study within the time limit.
1. Give ample time to the main point of the passage.
2. Don't get bogged down in unimportant details; keep the discussion moving.
3. Be prepared and sensitive enough to depart from your study and deal with real problems in individuals' lives.
☐ Summarize from time to time and at the end.
1. State clearly and concisely the points the group has discovered.
2. Emphasize the main point of the passage that the discussion brought out.
3. Don't use the summary to give the group information you did not get into the study. Do this only if you are short of time and want to cover a point.
4. Emphasize the specific applications and plans of action which the group came to because of the study.
☐ Help members make specific applications from the study to their own lives or to your group life. Your questions should lead you to this. Allow time for sharing and prayer.
☐ Before ending the study, give a brief introduction to next week's study.

Small Group Covenants
■ Definition: What a covenant is not and what it is
□ It is not a statement of what an ideal small group should be.
□ It is a statement of the steps this group is willing to take for the growth and edification of the members and for their equipping to do the work of ministry to the glory of God.

■ Reasons for covenanting
□ It puts love into action: "Let us consider how to stir up one another to love and good works" (Heb 10:24).
□ It establishes the intention of the group.
□ It defines expectations.
□ It provides accountability.
□ It enhances commitment.
□ It provides a basis for vulnerability.
□ It serves as a reference for evaluating.

■ When to covenant
□ When the group reaches or approaches the action stage
□ When the level of trust is growing
□ When the leader is considered a member of the group

■ Writing the covenant
□ Steps involved
   1. Ask the group to list what their expectations are for the group.
   2. As they share these, list them so that the whole group can see them.
   3. List what members have liked and disliked in other groups they have participated in or heard about.
   4. Ask what they are willing to commit themselves to as a group to meet their expectations. Make sure all agree with each statement and that each part is fully understood by all.
   5. State how long the covenant will be in force and when it will be evaluated.
   6. Have the covenant typed and signed by each member. Give a copy to each member.
   7. Follow through with encouragement, needed training and evaluation.
□ Content. For a small group to grow in each of the four components, steps must be taken for each. Suggestions for content include the following:
   1. Nurture—
   □ Personal disciplines outside the group—preparation, quiet time and so on.
   □ Attendance at other events as a group—conferences, seminars and so on.
   □ Bible study—what to study, who will lead.
   □ Books to read and discuss; tapes to listen to.

2. Worship—
☐ How much at a meeting.
☐ What forms to use.
☐ Who will lead.
3. Community—
☐ Attendance expected; ways of being accountable.
☐ Membership—who can join and when.
☐ Identifying and using gifts.
☐ Duration of this covenant.
☐ Length of meeting; content for sharing; fun activities.
☐ Prayer partnerships.
4. Mission—
☐ Training needed.
☐ What to pray for regularly.
☐ Information needed.
☐ Evangelism.
☐ Social action.
☐ Role in worldwide mission.

Evaluating Yourself and the Group

The following evaluation may help you think through your thoughts on the group before you do small group evaluation. Each member of the group should fill this out and then discuss what they have written.[1]

■ Check your participation as honestly as you can.   I . . .

_____ did not participate	_____ argued
_____ expressed my opinion	_____ had to have my way
_____ got my way	_____ could not get interested
_____ gave in	_____ felt hurt
_____ worked it out	_____ helped others work it out
_____ saw new possibilities	_____ was open to what others thought
_____ felt change was not necessary	_____ felt "they" were changing "my" group

■ Check how well the group functioned:

	No	Barely	Fairly Well	With Enthusiasm
All members participated.	_____	_____	_____	_____
The others listened and were open to what others thought.	_____	_____	_____	_____
Members supported one another.	_____	_____	_____	_____
We worked out differences of opinion openly.	_____	_____	_____	_____
We approached the matter sincerely.	_____	_____	_____	_____
We used the time wisely.	_____	_____	_____	_____
Our task was accomplished.	_____	_____	_____	_____

■ Check list for informal roles
Chapter five discussed the varying roles individuals take as informal leaders of the group. Check from below the roles you took during your small group meetings.[2] List ways which demonstrated your taking this role. Then do the same thing for one another, sharing your findings.

	1. Encouraged others to speak by . . .
―――――――	1. Encouraged others to speak by . . .
―――――――	2. Raised questions like . . .
―――――――	3. Played judge when I . . .
―――――――	4. Was sensitive to someone else by . . .
―――――――	5. Doodled during . . .
―――――――	6. Supported someone by . . .
―――――――	7. Recalled what was done earlier by saying . . .
―――――――	8. Dominated when I . . .
―――――――	9. Suggested a new idea, such as . . .
―――――――	10. Tried to encourage harmony between . . .
―――――――	11. Blocked action because . . .
―――――――	12. Helped move discussion toward a decision by . . .
―――――――	13. Reminded the members that . . .
―――――――	14. Tried to solve differences by . . .
―――――――	15. Gave information and opinions of . . .
―――――――	16. Played the hero when . . .
―――――――	17. Clarified a meaning when . . .
―――――――	18. Summarized information for . . .

■ Evaluating group interaction through roles
If you checked 1, 2, 7, 9, 12, 15, 17 and 18, you made efforts to *get the job done.* To move forward the group must be reviewed regularly, plans for development must be made, means to implement the plans must be provided, and evaluation and progress must be checked. By your personal role in the group you can directly and effectively help the group do its work.

Your efforts to *help people work together as a group* are indicated by 4, 6, 10 and 14. A group will be united and strong only if its members show concern for one another. Did all members participate, either providing information, making sure information is understood, bringing additional insight or identifying points to help bring the discussion to a decision? Were all suggestions considered? Were disagreements worked out to the satisfaction of the group as well as of the individuals having a different opinion? Did some persons keep the discussion on course? Was time spent wisely? A healthy, well-functioning group is one in which the members work together by giving, taking and blending ideas into workable plans and solutions.

In circling 3, 5, 8, 11, 13 and 16, you have indicated that you and your group may *have problems*. You and others in your group probably have not accepted your roles or feel that others have not accepted you. Make a special effort to get to know the other members better and give them the opportunity to know you better. Participate actively and encourage the other members to do so too.[3]

■ Evaluation of small group life as a whole
Think through strengths and weaknesses of your small group. Using the rating scale below, check your response. After everyone has finished, share your results together in the group.

1 Excellent   2 Good   3 Average   4 Fair   5 Poor

Items	Ratings				
1. Size of group	1	2	3	4	5
2. Use of time	1	2	3	4	5
3. Leadership	1	2	3	4	5
4. Materials used	1	2	3	4	5
5. Relationships with each other	1	2	3	4	5
6. Climate of trust	1	2	3	4	5
7. Freedom to be oneself	1	2	3	4	5
8. Communication of ideas	1	2	3	4	5
9. Communication of feelings	1	2	3	4	5
10. Acceptance of each other's faults	1	2	3	4	5
11. Concern for others' struggles	1	2	3	4	5
12. Understanding of Bible passages	1	2	3	4	5
13. Application of Scripture to daily life	1	2	3	4	5
14. Prayer	1	2	3	4	5
15. Outreach	1	2	3	4	5
16. Group confrontation with Christ	1	2	3	4	5
17. Personal growth within the group	1	2	3	4	5
18. Worship life of the group	1	2	3	4	5

Again, fill out your responses individually and then share with the group:
☐ The strong points of our group are
    1.

    2.

    3.

☐ The problems we need to work through together are
    1.

    2.

    3.

☐ The group has helped me
    1.

    2.

    3.

SMALL GROUP SUMMARY SHEET

Leader should fill out this quarterly for review and evaluation and for discussion with church's small group coordinator.

Leader _____
Address _____

For quarter ending _____
Small group meeting day _____ Time _____

Phone _____
(home) _____ (business)

Small group activities: What is our group doing in each area?

Nurture	Worship	Community	Mission

Member	Areas where member is growing	Areas where member desires more growth	Programs, studies, etc., which may help
1. _____	_____	_____	_____
2. _____	_____	_____	_____
3. _____	_____	_____	_____
4. _____	_____	_____	_____
5. _____	_____	_____	_____
6. _____	_____	_____	_____
7. _____	_____	_____	_____
8. _____	_____	_____	_____

Involving Others in Leadership

Involve members of your group in planning and leading the meetings. If someone leads music better than you, great! Talk with her about the meeting and what type of music may fit in. Let her lead that segment. Is there someone with a prayer ministry? Share with him the thrust of this week's meeting. Have him lead the group into a few minutes of thinking about why we are praying, mentioning things to pray about this week. Then pray. Ask someone you think can lead a good Bible discussion to colead with you a couple times. Prepare with that person. After several times let him take the main lead in the study.

Below are ideas for training a leader on a one-to-one basis and for a small group leadership training program in your church.

■ Training others to lead
☐ Look for Christians in your group who
   1. desire to grow as disciples
   2. have a commitment to your small group
   3. seem open and teachable
   4. contribute in the group but are also able to listen to others
☐ Spend time together outside of the group. Get to know each other, sharing thoughts, feelings, joys and questions. Listen, share, keep confidences.
☐ As you meet together, gradually share your vision for the small group. Ask for their feedback on the group, and share some of your thoughts and goals about group life.
☐ If they have not developed a consistent time alone each day with God, share your experience of doing so with them and help them embark.
☐ Pray together for the group and for your roles in the group. Be praying for new leaders on your own.
☐ Invite them to spend time with you as you prepare for the small group meeting. Talk about your plans for the week and how you will pull together the components. Prepare the Bible study together; begin to explain inductive Bible study (see Nurture Resources).
☐ Begin to let them lead parts of the group meeting. As you spend more time preparing and studying together, let them eventually lead the study and then have a major role in putting together and leading a whole meeting. Preparing together continues to give you time to share, evaluate and help each other grow. You'll be sharing some attitudes and values important in leading a group in the process.
☐ Encourage them to meet with at least one or two other people in the group, getting to know them and encouraging them.
☐ After several weeks they should see a small group as an evangelizing fellowship. If this has not been stated specifically, do so as you continue to talk about small groups.
☐ Encourage further training, such as the leadership training in your congrega-

tion or any other helpful conferences or seminars. Attend with them.

☐ Be sure each new leader knows the God who says, "Fear not, for I am with you!" God is the one on whom we depend.

☐ As they begin to lead your small group, part of your group or a new group, continue to encourage and pray. Suggest they begin meeting with someone whom they can train.

■ A congregational training program

Churches have found it helpful to do more in training their leaders than simply to have them read a book on leading groups. The learning experience of leaders has been enhanced when they can experience some of the content as well as have time to dialog about it. We would like to suggest the following means to help you train leaders for your small groups.

The leaders should receive some training before the groups start, so a strong beginning can be planned for in each group. This avoids the problem of a weak start and losing members right away. A strong start by groups helps keep members involved and committed.

Provide church members with materials and books on groups. They will not remember everything they read, but the general vision for small groups will start growing. It takes away some initial anxiety of not knowing the what and why of small groups.

Both gradual training (weekly) and intensive training (weekend) have been used successfully. It seems, however, that some gradual time is needed to process the content and experience some of the ideas. The two together (a weekend to start things out, with weekly meetings following) can capture the best of both worlds. Variety is good: use some lecture, some small group discussions, some question/answer time, and some simulated exercises.

This book has been targeted to a church audience. The *Small Group Leaders' Handbook* (InterVarsity Press) has been targeted to Inter-Varsity chapters on campus. The materials are different, but the books complement each other well and are easily adaptable to a variety of settings. Use them together. Chapters 4, 6, 7, 8, 10 and 11 from the *Small Group Leaders' Handbook* complement this book especially well.

☐ Your training curriculum should include the following:
1. Building a vision for small groups in our church
2. The place of small groups in our church
3. The forgiveness of Christ and our life together
4. How to study the Bible
5. Leading a group Bible study
6. Nurture—what, why, how
7. Worship—what, why, how
8. Community—what, why, how

    9. Mission—what, why, how
  10. You, the leader
  11. Leading others
  12. Communication—one-to-one and small group
  13. Starting a small group
  14. Stages of a small group
  15. Troubleshooting in small groups
  16. Planning small group meetings
  17. Training others in your small group

☐ A weekend training could follow this curriculum:
  1. Building a vision for small groups in our church
  2. The place of small groups in our church (Small groups meet to discuss.)
  3. How to study the Bible (Small group meeting with the four components—experienced leader leads the Bible study.)
  4. Leading a group Bible study
  5. Starting a small group (Have people share how they have started other groups; what principles are applicable here?)
  6. Planning a small group meeting (All leaders make a sample plan for four consecutive meetings.)
  7. You, the leader

☐ Weeknight training to follow the weekend:
  1. The place of the four components of small group life and how to lead each; commitment
  2. Communication and conflict resolution
  3. Leading others; training others in your small group
  4. Stages of small groups
  5. Troubleshooting

☐ One church's timetable:
  1. Weekend training
  2. Six weeks during which small group leaders meet together in small groups to experience group life and receive more training
  3. Each leader starting own group within four weeks of end of training
  4. Periodic meetings with all leaders
  5. Yearly follow-up training of old leaders and training for new leaders

Job Description: Small Group Coordinator

■ A primary task of the small group coordinator is to encourage formation and continued growth of small groups within the church. In addition to the small group leader's qualifications, the coordinator should

☐ Show evidence of a maturing witness for Jesus Christ and of living in practical obedience to his commands

☐ Have an appreciation for God's work through small groups

☐ Be part of a small group

☐ Be able to teach younger Christians how to study the Bible

☐ Be able to lead Bible studies

☐ Shepherd small group members

☐ Be willing to receive further training

   1. Meet with the pastor as needed

   2. Attend small group leadership training events

   3. Read materials related to group dynamics and leadership

■ The small group coordinator will

☐ Care for the small group leaders

☐ Have personal contact with each small group leader on a regular basis

☐ Care for the individual leader's personal growth and needs

☐ Discuss the use of the four components in the group

☐ Encourage the group leader, praying with him or her

☐ Pray at least weekly for each small group leader by name

☐ Meet corporately (perhaps every other month) with the small group leaders for whom responsible in order to

   1. Discuss the current situation of each small group

   2. Facilitate the leaders' understanding and dealings with problems in their groups

   3. Share ideas or resources and pray together

☐ Help plan, conduct and evaluate training of small group leaders

☐ Assist leaders in selecting and training new leaders from existing groups

■ Small group coordinators also serve as liaisons between the leaders and the pastors by

☐ Helping small groups meet members' immediate needs, such as hospital visitation

☐ Seeing that all reports are turned in and that responsibilities are being met

☐ Serving as a member of the church committee responsible for small groups

☐ Facilitating understanding of the place of small groups in the life of congregation

☐ Transmitting the pastor's and elders' vision for the church to the small group leaders

Chapter 14
Nurture Resources

Bible study will probably be the main nurture source for your group. But don't let your creativity in planning stop here. Vary the kind of study you do over a period of time. Include an inductive study of passages on similar topics, a character study, a study of a book of the Bible, a study using a guide. Help on preparing these is provided in chapter thirteen, Leadership Resources. The first section of Nurture Resources will be an actual Bible study lesson, one we've prepared for use in one of your first small group meetings. Following the guide is a section listing other Bible study guides appropriate for group use.

Although Bible study may be your main nurture experience, feel free to use one or two weeks between studies to do something different. The third section suggests other nurturing activities for occasional use.

A Bible Study: Basic Elements of Christian Group Life (Acts 2:41-47)

■ Purpose of the study: To help group members see a biblical example of community, nurture, worship and mission in operation in the early church.

■ Background and introduction
□ Acts 2:1-12 tells what happened on the day of Pentecost when the believers
were all filled with the Holy Spirit and spoke the mighty works of God in a variety
of languages. Acts 2:14-40 is Peter's evangelistic sermon to the cosmopolitan
crowd in Jerusalem. He challenges them to believe in Jesus, repent and save
themselves from the "crooked generation."
□ In the passage we are studying (Acts 2:41-47), we will see what characterizes
the *new generation* of believers. From this example, we hope to learn what should
happen in our life together in a small group.
□ Read Acts 2:41-47.

■ Questions
In the study, several questions are grouped together. These are all aimed at
getting at a main point and applying it. If your group has answered or responded
to several of the questions in the set, skip the others. If not, the additional
questions can be used to help members probe for facts, interpretation and application.
□ Summarize in your own words what their fellowship (koinonia) was like.
□ How might the group life in the early church have been in sharp contrast to
the "crooked generation" they were being saved from? Why was it different?
□ How might being in a small group with other Christians help you to be saved
from this crooked generation? In what sense can a small group of Christians live
a contrasting lifestyle from other lifestyles in today's society?
□ Read verse 42. How did the new converts express their *commitment?* What is
meant by the phrase "they *devoted* themselves to . . ."? What does their devotion
tell you about the foundation of their life together? To what things in your life
are you most devoted? How can we increase our commitment to the things
mentioned in verse 42? What experiences have any of you had in other small
groups where a strong commitment was evidenced?
□ Reread verses 43-47. Note the last sentence: "And the Lord added to their
number day by day those who were being saved." What could the non-Christians
have observed in the Christian community which drew them to salvation? How
did the believers regard their earthly possessions? How might this have been a
sign of true conversion to the outsiders? Would you consider these people richer
or poorer for believing in Christ? Why?
□ Look at verse 47 again. How would you compare God's role in salvation with
the role of Christians in evangelism?
□ What changes in lifestyle do we need to make to be a clearer sign to outsiders

that Christ has made a difference in our life?

☐ Share the name of a friend whom you hope God will add to the Christian fellowship. Pray for those named.

■ Summary

☐ The group of early Christians were committed to the apostles' teaching, which we now have in the New Testament. Study of the apostles' teaching provides *nurture* for our small group.

☐ They were also devoted to fellowship (koinonia). They broke bread together, prayed together, shared possessions and met in each other's homes. This is a biblical example of *community* life which we hope to follow.

☐ We also observed their commitment to regular *worship*. They daily attended the Temple; they ate with glad and generous hearts, *praising God!* We want to learn to worship as they did.

☐ *Mission* was a natural result of their life together. Signs and wonders were done; they had favor with all the people; "and the Lord added to their number day by day those who were being saved."

Study Guides on Books of the Bible

FBS: Fisherman Bible Study guides, published by Harold Shaw Publishers, P.O.
    Box 567, Wheaton, IL 60187
IVP: InterVarsity Press, P.O. Box 1400, Downers Grove, IL 60515
LBS: LifeBuilder Bible Studies, published by InterVarsity Press.
NBS: Neighborhood Bible Studies, distributed by Tyndale House Publishers, 336
    Gundersen Drive, Wheaton, IL 60187

☐ Genesis   Genesis (LBS)
                               Genesis 1—25 (FBS)
                               Genesis 25—50 (FBS)
                               Genesis (NBS)
☐ Exodus   Moses: A Man Changed by God (IVP)
☐ 1 Samuel   David, Vol. 1 (FBS)
☐ 2 Samuel   David, Vol. 2 (FBS)
☐ Psalms   Psalms (FBS)
                               Psalms and Proverbs (NBS)
☐ Proverbs   Proverbs and Parables (FBS)
                               Psalms and Proverbs (FBS)
☐ Ecclesiastes   Ecclesiastes (FBS)
☐ Daniel   Daniel (LBS, 1986)
☐ Amos   Amos (NBS)
                               Amos (FBS)
☐ Habakkuk   Just Living by Faith (IVP)
☐ Matthew   The God Who Understands Me (FBS)
                               Matthew, Book 1 (NBS)
                               Matthew, Book 2 (NBS)
☐ Mark   Mark (LBS)
                               Mark (NBS)
                               Mark (FBS)
☐ Luke   Luke (NBS)
☐ John   John (FBS)
                               John, Book 1 (NBS)
                               John, Book 2 (NBS)
                               Lifestyle of Love (IVP)
☐ Acts   Acts (NBS)
                               Acts 1—12 (FBS)
                               Acts 13—28 (FBS)
☐ Romans   Romans (LBS, 1986)
                               Romans (NBS)
                               Romans (FBS)
☐ 1 Corinthians   1 Corinthians (NBS)

	1 Corinthians (FBS)
☐ 2 Corinthians	2 Corinthians and Galatians (NBS)
☐ Galatians	Galatians (LBS, 1986)
	2 Corinthians and Galatians (NBS)
☐ Ephesians	Ephesians (LBS)
	Ephesians (FBS)
	Ephesians and Philemon (NBS)
☐ Philippians	Philippians (LBS)
	Philippians (FBS)
	Philippians and Colossians (NBS)
☐ Colossians	Philippians and Colossians (NBS)
☐ 1 Thessalonians	Letters to Thessalonians (FBS)
☐ 2 Thessalonians	Letters to Thessalonians (FBS)
☐ 1 Timothy	Letters for Reluctant Leaders (IVP)
	Letters to Timothy (FBS)
☐ 2 Timothy	Letters for Reluctant Leaders (IVP)
	Letters to Timothy (FBS)
☐ Philemon	Ephesians and Philemon (NBS)
☐ Hebrews	Hebrews (NBS)
	Hebrews (FBS)
☐ James	Faith That Works (IVP)
	1 John and James (NBS)
	James (FBS)
☐ 1 Peter	1 and 2 Peter (NBS)
☐ 2 Peter	1 and 2 Peter (NBS)
☐ 1 John	1 John and James (NBS)
☐ Revelation	Revelation (FBS)

Other Ideas That Nurture
■ Scripture memory
☐ Do a psalm a month.
☐ Memorize one verse or passage from the book you are studying.
☐ Use *Scripture Memory 101* (IVP) or *Topical Memory System* (NavPress, P.O. Box 20, Colorado Springs, CO 80901).

■ Hymn study
☐ Take a hymn which has good theology and content in it. Sing it, study it, sing it again.
☐ List ideas about God or outline the structure, noting repeated ideas, themes in the song and why it holds together.
☐ Use the Scripture listed with the hymn, if any.
☐ Sing it in unison, in parts, read one verse and so on. This could be particularly

helpful on an evening when you want a shorter nurture time.
□ Good books are available on the background of hymns (see Nurture bibliography). Check your church or public library.

■ Sermon reflection
Discuss the sermon from the previous Sunday. (Warn your members ahead about this so they can take notes or at least tune in closely!) If available, secure a tape of the sermon and play parts of it at your meeting.
□ What was the main point?
□ How did this emphasis come out of the Scripture text used? Look at the text together.
□ What other ideas were used to emphasize or support this idea?
□ What application was being made for our individual lives? our congregational life?
□ How can we individually or corporately act on this?
If you want your group to do immediate reflection, you may want to have brunch together after the service to discuss the sermon and its implications.

■ Preparation for hearing sermon
Find out the text the pastor will use next Sunday for the sermon. Study this passage together as a group.

■ Book study with application
□ Read a book together and discuss it, perhaps a chapter or section a week.
□ If you meet less than once a week, you may want to take a whole book, reading it and discussing it at a meeting. This helps you get the author's whole perspective before you talk about the book.
□ Think through how you can apply what you have learned—in your own life, in your small group, in your congregation, in your community, in the world. Pray for one another.
□ Plan for your small group to take some action. One small group, after reading a book on energy use, discussed the stewardship of God's resources. They encouraged church members to bike, car-pool and walk to church. One specific Sunday was set aside for emphasis on this theme.

■ Book reports
Have a night where each member shares the book that has most influenced his or her life. Tell what the book is about, what impact it had on you and why you like it. Many will find new reading material out of this exercise.

■ Magazine article
Read an article from a magazine together. If it is long, you may want to have it

read before the meeting. Choose a few questions to help the group start discussing
the topic.

■ Tapes
Listen to a tape and have four or five questions ready for discussion. These should
be used with discretion. *Always* preview carefully. Most groups would rather talk
themselves than spend time listening to tapes. You can order tapes on a wide
range of topics from IVP. Write for an order form. Your church library may also
have several good tapes your small group could use.

■ Films
View a film as a small group. Get together afterward to talk about the main ideas
expressed in the film. Are the values and ideas consistent with a biblical perspective of life? How are the ideas similar to or different from our way of thinking?
What motivated the characters in the movie? You can think of other questions
which may fit specific films.

■ Community or church activity
Attend a church meeting, lecture or concert together. Gather afterward to discuss
the ideas presented and your responses. You can also do this by attending a retreat
or conference together (great for community building!).

■ Experience
Each of us has ways in which God has been working in us. We also have had
different experiences in dealing with doubt, pain, death, joy, love and so on. Share
these so that members can benefit and grow from each other's experience. Remember that one person's experience is not prescriptive of what every other
person's experience will or should be. God meets us as individuals. Sharing experiences can help us, not to prescribe cures, but to encourage one another.

Chapter 15
Worship Resources

Worship is praising and magnifying God by focusing on his nature and his actions. It is adoring him for who he is and loving him as our wonderful Father. The goal of worship is to bring joy to God. He is worthy of all praise and all glory, from all his creation. Worship involves our total life; what we express in formal ways must be borne out in our daily lives. The activities that follow suggest ways you might help your group focus on and worship God.

■ Psalms, hymns and songs

☐ Hymns at the beginning of your meeting can set the tone for your time together.

☐ Remind the group to think of themselves as speaking to God as they sing, to be more concerned with the content of the songs than the quality of their singing.

☐ Use songs which focus on the triune God, what he is like and what he has done. Use familiar songs and hymns at first. Keep a list of those the group knows.

☐ Read a song rather than sing it for a change of pace.

☐ Give background material if helpful for worship (see *Hymns That Live,* Worship bibliography). Have members concentrate on one or two main themes which run through the hymn. By pointing them out ahead, you can help them focus as they sing or read.

■ Praying

Praying is a natural part of worship. Prayer can take many forms, of which these are a few:

☐ Prayer bombardment: A topic can be introduced with members responding spontaneously with one word or a brief phrase which reflects what they are thinking about at that time. (Example—*Christ's presence:* "Our Lord." "You are here." "We adore you." Example—*attributes of God:* "goodness"; "love"; "mercy.")

☐ Litany: A prayer is prepared. The leader reads a brief portion, and the group responds as a whole. Each member needs a copy of the prayer. Hymns or a psalm can also be used in this way. A group member may want to write a litany which expresses the group's experiences and learning.

☐ Personalize the standard form: Take Psalm 23 or the Lord's Prayer and have each person write his or her own version during the week. Pray these during your next small group meeting.

☐ Conversational prayer: Each person prays freely in the group. You may want to ask for prayer requests and give suggestions so that people uncomfortable with this know what the prayer time is for.

☐ Chain prayer: Each person prays in order around the circle.

☐ Bible prayer: Look back at the passage you have studied and ask what attributes we see of God in this passage. Praise him for these aspects of his character and person.

☐ Prayer of thanks: Make sure that some of your sharing is rejoicing in the good things God has done for us. Enjoy the goodness of God together, hearing of his grace in each other's lives. Respond to God in praise during or after this time of sharing.

☐ Body worship: Work through prayer by allowing the group to express itself not only in words but also through their bodies. During confession, lie on your face; for praise, lift your hands; for petition, kneel. This may help members experience worship in a new way.

☐ Names of God: Ask your group to think of all the names that Scripture gives to God or Jesus. Why are they significant to members of the group? Make this a basis for your prayer and praise.

■ Books

☐ J. I. Packer's *Knowing God,* A. W. Tozer's *The Knowledge of the Holy* and J. B. Phillips's *Your God Is Too Small* are excellent choices. Read short excerpts which will direct your thoughts to God and give time for the group to respond in worship.

☐ Use books of prayer or responsive readings such as those of the church. These prayers and readings can open or close times of prayer. They also help demonstrate how great men and women of the faith have responded to the character of God in the past.

■ Writing

☐ Sometimes it is helpful to collect your thoughts and write them down. Think over the last day or two. List things for which you are thankful. Share your list with the group. Have members lead in prayer as they praise God with what they have written. Write letters of gratitude to God; share parts of them; pray them conversationally back to God.

☐ Creative writing can also be a help in worship. Give group members time to write a poem, song or psalm. Share and use as an introduction to worship.

■ Silence and meditation

☐ Often we think all our time in a group should be verbal. Take a few minutes to pray and meditate silently. (Placed at appropriate times, members may want to share after this time or begin to quietly talk again.)

☐ To prepare people for this experience it may be helpful to ask group members to close their eyes while one person reads Revelation 4. Group members should focus on being in the presence of God without feeling compelled to talk. Listen to God.

Chapter 16

Community Resources

Small group activities can enhance community life:
going on a weekend retreat; eating meals together; having a picnic; reading a book like *Winnie the Pooh* or a play like *The Man
Born to Be King,* each person taking a part; going on social outings
to plays, movies or concerts; making pizza or ice cream together;
playing a team game like volleyball.

These activities give you fun, relaxed time together. But they do
not necessarily give you more understanding and appreciation of
the other people in your group. These alone are not sufficient for
building up the body of Christ.

The rest of this chapter provides tools that can help you build
true Christian community. They are grouped according to the stage
at which each might be most helpful.

Exploration
■ "Who Am I?"

Make a list of eight items which identify who you are or which tell about significant aspects and roles of your life. (Examples: mother, son, friend, choir member, writer, critic, Sunday-school teacher.)

Then consider each item in your list. Try to imagine how it would be if that item were no longer true for you. (For example, if you were no longer a son or daughter, if you lost both parents: What would that mean to you? How would you feel? What would you do? What would your life be like?) After reviewing each item in this way, rank the items by putting a number to the right of each item. Order them according to the importance this role has to you at this time. Which would most drastically affect your life if it were taken away?

Finally, share your results with one person in your group. Tell each other how you came to your decisions. Be as open as you can. Then regather as a group. Discuss the following: Is there something about yourself this exercise has taught you? As you thought over the question of loss of an item, did you realize some things you hadn't before? What role was most significant for you? Why? Then let the person with whom you shared tell the group one thing he or she appreciated about you from your sharing.

■ Warm Up

Explain to the group that the following questions will help us get to know one another better. They are not "loaded," but simply represent a way to get to know each other in a short time.

Take one set of questions at a time. The leader can begin by answering first. Go around the circle, each person answering the same set of questions. Only when you've all answered Set 1 would you move to Set 2.

☐ Set 1

1. What is your name? (If you did this earlier, do it again so names can be learned quickly.)
2. Where did you live between the ages of seven and twelve?
3. What stands out most in your mind about the school you attended at that time?

☐ Set 2

1. How many brothers and sisters were in your family during the ages of seven to twelve?
2. How did you like to get warm when you were chilled or cold as a child? Perhaps after an afternoon of skating, skiing or sledding? Or early mornings at a cabin or out camping?

☐ Set 3

During your childhood where did you feel the center of human warmth was? Was it a room or a person? (For example, the TV room when your family was all together? the kitchen?) It may not have been a room at all; it may have been a person around whom you sensed safeness and warmth. (The leader may want to mention that some people do not remember a center of human warmth in the home. This will put at ease people for whom this was true.) Was there another center of warmth for them?

☐ Set 4

This question is asked to the group as a whole and you do not need to go in a round for this (Let people answer as they feel comfortable; some may choose not to answer at this time): When in your life, if ever, did God become more than a word? When did he become a living being, someone who was alive in your own thinking?

This may not be an account of a conversion. This transition in one's thinking can happen before actual conversion or after. It may have happened in conversation with a person who loved them, in a worship service or in listening to music. This is not a time of discovering the whole counsel of God, but simply a time of personal awareness.

As you conclude this discussion, point out in summary how our different experiences bring us to different points in our growth and our experiences. Although our security and acceptance begin with physical warmth and graduate to human warmth, we are never complete until we find security in God.

☐ *Note:* If time is short and this is not your first meeting, omit Set 1 and the first question in Set 2.

■ Twenty Loves

☐ Give each person a piece of paper. Allow a few minutes for all group members to list twenty activities they enjoy doing. Some may find they have far more than twenty; others may have trouble listing five. Encourage them to think about what they enjoy doing most. For some that may even be daydreaming.

☐ After they have made their lists, have each make the following notations next to each item to which it applies:

(A)   Those things which you prefer to do alone

(P)   Things you prefer to do with other people; if others are involved, put names of others with whom you most enjoy this activity

($)   Those which cost money to do (over $1.00)

(R)   Items which have some element of risk involved (physical or personal)

(S)   Those activities which are sedentary (more quiet or passive)

(M)   Those which are active

(C)   Things which take some form of communication to do

(L)   Items you had to learn to do, a skill you had to acquire

(CH) Activities you did as a child

(PA) Activities that at least one of your parents does or did

☐ Look at your list and rank the activities in order of preference. What do you notice about yourself? What aspects come out repeatedly, particularly in your top five? Is there anything you hadn't realized before?

☐ Now ask yourself more specific questions:

1. Do you most enjoy doing things by yourself, with others, or both? If with others, are there people you continually enjoy being with—friends? family? members of the same sex? members of the opposite sex? Are there people you consistently enjoy doing a variety of things with? Do you usually enjoy one-to-one time, small groups or large groups?

2. Do the things you enjoy usually cost money?

3. Are you a risk taker? What kind?

4. Are you sedentary, active or a mixture?

5. Do you do many things that require communication? Are you often with people doing things that don't require communication?

6. Did you have to work at skills to do the things you enjoy? Are those items in your top five or lower on your scale? Or have you most enjoyed things which you can do naturally?

7. Are you enjoying things you learned as a child and that your parents did? What things have changed since childhood? What has been built on?

8. Looking at your list, which would be hardest for you to give up? Which would you miss the most if you didn't do it?

☐ Take about ten minutes to discuss your findings with one other person in the group. (If those in the group know each other fairly well, you could stay together.) When the group pulls back together, share with the whole group what you saw about yourself, particularly if you saw something you hadn't realized or thought about before. Have each person say at least one thing he or she particularly enjoyed learning in talking with his or her partner.

☐ *Note:* There are no good or bad answers in this exercise. The purpose is simply to see ourselves and to share what we see with others.

■ Fire Drill

Your house is on fire. Your family members are all safe. You have thirty seconds to run through the house and collect three to four articles you would want to save. Allow one minute for each member to write down what those things would be. Let each person tell the items on their list and why they chose each. After everyone has shared, discuss what people learned about the things they value.

■ Pocketbook Probe

Each person takes his or her wallet out and lays it on the table, allowing others to pick it up and look through it. Spend time hearing what new things you've learned about one another. To increase the input, you could take out everything in your pockets or purse.

■ Pictures

Each member brings five to ten pictures or slides (preferably slides which can be shown to the whole group at the same time) which depict characteristics about them. It may show favorite vacation spots, an activity they like to do (such as gardening), or people meaningful to them. Take turns showing the pictures and explaining their importance.

■ "What Would You Do If . . ."

Give each member a piece of paper with a statement on it. Announce that the first part of everyone's sentence is "What would you do if . . ." Let the group think about their answers and then go in a circle to hear responses. Examples of statements on the paper:

☐ "you could take an extra day off work?"
☐ "you could go anywhere in the world?"
☐ "you could become some animal for a day?"
☐ "a picture you were looking at came to life?"
☐ "a plant attacked you?"

Make up your own endings.

Exploration and Transition
■ Sharing Questions (*which* stage depends on the question being used)
A sharing question is an open-ended sentence which gives individuals a chance to say something about themselves. The type of question you ask will depend on the developmental stage of the group. History-giving questions (What was your favorite subject in school?) are probably most appropriate to the exploration stage. Questions that would deal with our group life and feelings about the group would help the group most during later transition and action stages.

Allow people to pass if they are not comfortable responding to the question at this time. It's better than their manufacturing an answer. Here are some sample questions:

☐ What was the high point and the low point of this week for you? (exploration or early transition)

☐ What person in this group do you identify with most and why? (transition and action)

☐ If you had a free day and could do anything you wanted (no restrictions), what would you do? (exploration)

☐ Describe an experience where the Holy Spirit has been your Comforter. (transition)

☐ What personal relationship are you really enjoying in your life right now? What personal relationship in your life would you like to make better? (transition and action)

Questions or statements which give other members personal affirmation can be used at times of termination or celebration: What is one thing you appreciate about each member of this group? How have you been encouraged by a member or members of this group? (So that one person—the encourager—doesn't get all the feedback on this, combine it with other similar questions such as those who have taught or served.)

These are only a few of hundreds of questions you could use. Pick those which are appropriate to your group and will help them share.

■ Guess Who
Each member writes the answer to the following questions on a piece of paper.
☐ What was your favorite TV (or radio) program when you were a child?
☐ What is your favorite color?
☐ Where would you like to spend a vacation?
☐ What one word best describes your life right now?
Fold the paper in half and put in a bowl. Have one person pick a piece of paper and read the answers. The group then tries to decide which person in the group would have answered in that way, giving their reasons for that guess. The person it describes can play along and guess others. After everyone has guessed, the person who wrote the answers can explain the answers. Repeat this procedure

until you have removed all of the slips and tried to guess each one.

■ True/False
☐ Have all members write four statements about themselves on a piece of paper, three of them true and one false. Each should be plausible. Do not label which is true and which is false. Example:
    I wish I had the nerve to hang glide.
    I have vacationed in Japan.
    I hate squash!
    My career dream was to be president of a college.
☐ Going in a circle, have each person read their statements. The group members then guess which is the false statement and tell why they chose that one. See if your group can reach consensus. After a few minutes let the person tell which were true and which one false.

■ Childhood Table and Now
☐ All members take a piece of paper and draw on it the shape of the table where they ate most of their meals as a child. Now think of your family at that time (say, around 9-12 years old). Place each family member at the table at the place where he or she usually sat, writing his name and the color which best characterizes him to you at that time. Write on the table the color which describes the overall mood. Draw in lines showing where main communication took place.
☐ Draw a second table. If those same members of your family were together today, what colors would you give them? Place them in the same places with today's colors, an overall color and lines of communication. Have members of the group share their tables with the rest of the group.

■ Journey of Faith
Each member of the group draws a line graph which illustrates his or her pilgrimage of faith in the Christian life. It will probably have high points, low points, leveling-off times, or whatever seems to best depict what was happening at that time. Have members share their graph with the group, explaining what it means and how their life in Christ was affected (or perhaps how the living Christ affected them).

■ Coat of Arms

In the past, a coat of arms told something about a person or his family by symbolism. Make your own coat of arms, describing things about yourself. Write your answers in the appropriate spaces, or, for those creative people, draw them.

☐ Upper left: Two things you do well.

☐ Middle left: Your most satisfying experience or achievement.

☐ Lower left: What you would do with one year left to live.

☐ Upper right: "Psychological home" or place where you feel most at home.

☐ Middle right: Three people most influential in your life or who mean the most to you.

☐ Lower right: Three words you would like said about you.

Share your coat of arms with the group.

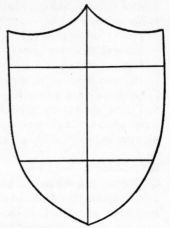

Transition

■ A Round

A round is giving each member in the group 30 seconds to share how he or she is feeling right now. (Go in a circle.) It may be used at the beginning of any group session or at the end. It is designed to be a short status report. No feedback or evaluation of one another is allowed. After everyone has shared, the group has the option of following up or asking clarification of a group member. A short, quick round may do several things for a group:

☐ Members become more aware of their feelings.

☐ They learn to report feelings (emotions) without evaluation.

☐ Hidden agendas that may otherwise hinder the group process may come into the open, or unfinished business at the end of a meeting may be discovered.

☐ Openness and freedom to share may become a natural part of group experience with this warm-up.

☐ It can help in transition when people may need encouragement to share.

■ Weather Report

Adapt the "round" by having members report their feelings in weather terminology—partly cloudy, sunny and so on. This can often be helpful for people who have trouble using feeling words.

Transition and Action
◼ Strength Bombardment
This exercise is designed to let you express the positive feelings you have for each other by pointing out the strengths you see in others. This is best done after you have gotten to know each other fairly well.

☐ Ask one person to remain silent while the others concentrate on this person and "bombard" him or her with all the things that they like about him or her or see as a strength. Keep bombarding the first person with positive feelings until you run out of words.

☐ Now move on to the next person in your group and do the same—until you have covered everyone in your group.

☐ After everyone has had a turn, ask, "How did you feel when you were the focus of bombardment? Don't evaluate what was said about you, but tell how you felt about getting the feedback." Then ask, "How did you feel about giving feedback to others?"

◼ Values Experience
Ask each person to share a situation from the last week (two weeks, month) where one of their values (or something valued highly) was either threatened or affirmed. *Variation:* Ask each person to share a time when he or she felt a value (or something highly prized) was either threatened or affirmed *in this group.*

◼ Color Me
As your group members feel closer to one another, you may need to encourage them to share those feelings.

☐ Each person should think of a color he or she would use to describe every other person in the group.

☐ Take a piece of paper and put your name on the top. Pass the paper randomly so that each person can put the color he or she associates with you on it. Then return the sheet to the person whose name is on the top.

☐ Let one person at a time respond to the colors they've been given. Give the rest a chance to explain why they gave a certain color, particularly if it differs from what others have given.

☐ Each can ask for clarification as needed.

If you want to be more direct, you could ask what feeling you have when you think of each individual person in your group. Then go around and give this feedback. If there are feelings which need to be worked on—hurt, distance, hostility—talk about it and confront the problems. If your group is ready for this, it could move into very close community and move you to action.

◼ Strengths and Abilities
Identify specific strengths and abilities you see in each individual in the group.

Give specific instances when you have noticed these in the group. How has this person used these gifts? How would you like to encourage them to continue with their use? Do this for each person in your group.

Termination
■ Gift Giving
This group experience is particularly good for a closing time of sharing and caring. It is also suited for times of review and celebration.

☐ Have one person sit in the center of your small group circle. Members, one at a time, then give to this person an intangible gift or Bible verse which reflects something they would like to see him or her have or an area where they would like to see growth. Perhaps they will offer a reminder of a special time or quality. Give the gift and explain why you are giving that gift.

☐ Each member of the group takes turns being in the center.

☐ Close with a time of thanksgiving and prayer for one another. You may want to lay hands on each person as you pray for them.

Body-life Fellowship for Any Stage
■ Passing the Peace
At the end of a meeting you may want to gather in a circle, join hands and pass the words of the benediction around the group: "May the peace of Christ go with you, Jim." The recipient will respond, "And also with you, Mary." This may be used at the end of a retreat or perhaps a study where there has been significant sharing.

■ Prayer Partners
A prayer partner is a member of your group with whom you meet regularly for sharing and prayer. If your group meets every other week, you may want to meet the week your group does not. To begin with, you may want to use some sharing questions to get to know each other. Sharing significant parts in one's life with one person in the group often begins to help us build trust with the group as a whole. It also gives each of us the opportunity for a more in-depth relationship than we can likely build with six others.

Chapter 17
Mission Resources

Ideas for what we can do to love our world, our neighbors, are as broad as the needs that exist. The suggestions that follow are just a few of the possibilities, but they may serve as pump primers.

The ideas are grouped to some extent by type of ministry. But each could easily belong in another group. We are *whole* people, and those we serve in the name of Christ are whole as well. When you visit a shut-in for Christ's sake, you can call it social concern, pre-evangelism or even evangelism. Let the categories of ministry help you if they can, but don't let them bind your thinking.

Ministries of Grace to Society
■ Needs
☐ Share your concern for the needs (physical, spiritual, emotional) of those people you know. Pray for each other's friends and family during small group meetings. Discuss ways that might help meet some of those needs and encourage one another in love for others. Check back on those people for whom you pray.
☐ Work together as a group to meet needs of those you know—a moving crew for people moving in or out, meals for people in times of need (births, deaths, hospitalization of a family member), home repairs for elderly, child care. Keep your eyes and ears open. Pray for creative sensitivity to seeing needs around you that can be met by your group. A group can often do things one person cannot accomplish alone.

■ Neighborhood resources
☐ Have your small group compile a neighborhood resource sheet for the area around your church (or for your own neighborhood if you live a distance from the church). List frequently called numbers on the sheet: police and fire, schools, hospitals, poison center, weather conditions, main city and county offices and so on. Put the church name, address and phone number at the bottom.
☐ Distribute this to new neighbors and prospective members.
☐ If your small group members live in the same area, bring a meal to new neighbors and share the list with them. You may want to offer them additional advice on resources—piano teachers for children, nursery schools. In your small group, pray for the needs of these people, opening yourselves to help where you are able.

■ "Lord, when did we see thee . . . ?"
☐ Make regular visits to a nursing home, hospital, prison or mental hospital. Meet regularly with residents, perhaps ones who have few visitors.
☐ If it is allowed, conduct Bible studies, worship services or devotional programs with music, short readings or meditations for those who desire.
☐ Go Christmas caroling, Easter caroling or any other type of caroling for these lonely ones.
☐ Volunteer a day or regular time periods when you would assist at a food distribution center. An inner-city church may use you to serve a meal or assist with one of their programs.

■ International students
☐ Contact a local college or university and offer hospitality to international students.
☐ As a group, provide an introductory tour of your city, with a dinner afterward.
☐ Each family unit could adopt a student for the year, offering steady friendship.

■ Political awareness

☐ Discuss an article, book or your church's position on an issue that affects the poor. Or do a Bible study on justice and peace.

☐ Decide together what position you want to back as Christians.

☐ Write your representatives to make your views known.

■ World hunger awareness

☐ Find ways to keep awareness of the world's hungry before your congregation and community. Study the issue as a small group. Bring in a speaker to address the topic.

☐ Encourage one another and others in your church in lifestyle changes.

☐ Support groups dealing with the problem from a Christian perspective.

☐ Plan a hunger meal at your church.

☐ Use one day a week for fasting and prayer.

Ministries of Evangelism

■ Preparing for witness

☐ Sometimes the sound barrier is one of the biggest blocks to sharing our faith with others. During the first six weeks of your group, use the Journey of Faith in your small group (see Community Resources). This will give each member a chance to begin to talk about their faith with others. As it becomes more natural to discuss your faith in the small group, pray for opportunities to share with those outside your group.

☐ Pray for friends. Group members can share names of those with whom they desire to share more openly about Christ. Discuss how members could more effectively communicate the love of Christ.

☐ Encourage one another in witness. For your nurture time read a book that helps: *Out of the Saltshaker* (IVP) by Rebecca Pippert, or *Good News Is for Sharing* (David C. Cook) by Leighton Ford.

■ Witness!

Each week decide to take one more step toward your verbal witness to Jesus Christ. The following steps may help you break through the spiritual sound barrier on spiritual issues. Each member can do a step a week and report back at the next meeting.

☐ Initiate a light conversation with someone you don't know—at the grocery store, the golf course, a lunch counter, wherever.

☐ Say some words of encouragement to someone outside of your family.

☐ Have a significant conversation with one person you know well—something beyond the weather. Ask his or her ideas or feelings on a topic and express yours.

☐ Share with a friend something you have learned from the Bible, a sermon or teaching, a book or an article, that has affected your life.

☐ Ask one person what the church, God or Jesus means to them. *Listen.*

☐ Discuss with one significant other the needs in his or her life. How would God's presence help that person's life?

☐ Tell one person the difference Jesus Christ has made in your life.

☐ Ask one person to study a Gospel passage about Jesus with you.

☐ If you have done all of the above with Christians from your church, now take from the fourth step on and talk to someone who has made no profession of faith in Christ.

■ Group evangelism

☐ Plan a party or group outing for friends to stimulate further discussion of the gospel. Perhaps the small group could host a dinner, topical discussion, or a dessert following a spiritually provocative movie or play.

☐ Arrange for a literature distribution in the neighborhood. How about a book-table at the subway or commuter station?

☐ Start a series of investigative Bible studies for group members' friends.

Ministry within the Body

■ Sunday service

☐ Teach a class. Consider how you might serve your church through teaching a class together. Perhaps you could teach a five-week series, taking turns according to the gifts of each.

☐ Tape the worship service, sermons or talks. Your small group could take responsibility for your church's tape ministry. Tape the Sunday worship or perhaps just the sermon or a special series. Make tapes available to check out from your church library. Deliver copies to shut-ins who could listen to a tape recorder and hear Sunday services.

■ Discerning needs and caring

☐ If there is a program which your church or community would benefit from, have your small group establish and do the initial leadership of that program—a junior high ministry, a widow(er) support group, food distribution center, elderly assistance program, a divorcee support group, a support group for the unemployed.

☐ Shut-ins: Each small group could care for one shut-in from the church. You can send cards on birthdays and special occasions, provide a visit at least monthly, bring a meal and eat with them, bring families (children included) when appropriate. If there are many shut-ins in your church, each family unit could take one as their care-burden.

☐ Scholarships: Provide scholarships from your group for church members to receive summer training (camps, conferences, work projects), attend conventions (youth conventions, Urbana missionary conference), or various retreats held throughout the year. You need not limit it to youth!

■ Caring for missionaries and whole-church outreach

☐ Mission awareness: Attend your church's missions conference (local or national) together. Share while there what you are learning. When you return, discuss what action you can take as individuals or as a group to keep informed and active in world mission.

☐ Money for missions: Work together on a project which would raise extra money for missions. Often stores hire extra people to do a day of inventory or a large sale. Your group could work together that day, with the money going to a specific missionary, mission board or ministry.

☐ Adopt a country: Have each small group "adopt" a country. You may even want to name your group that country—"the Zimbabwe group." Learn whatever you can about the country, church activity there, outreach going on at present, response of the people and so on. Pray for the nationals and missionaries you know from your church in that country. Provide the whole congregation with relevant information regarding the country, mission work and prayer requests. Use channels like a newsletter, bulletin or bulletin boards. Keep up the mission awareness of the whole congregation.

☐ Adopt a missionary: Similar to the above, only you identify with a missionary or missionary family from your church. Find out specifically what type of work they do, ways to pray for them, special needs they have, and what their lifestyle is like. Send cards on special occasions; send letters to keep them informed about home activity. Do not expect them to be steady correspondents. They are busy. But ask them to keep you informed. You can pass that information on to the pastor and congregation as appropriate.

Notes

Chapter 3: The Four Ingredients of Good Group Life
[1]Rebecca M. Pippert, *Out of the Saltshaker* (Downers Grove, Ill.: InterVarsity Press, 1979).

Chapter 5: Sharing Leadership
[1]For a more extended discussion of these roles, see David W. Johnson and Frank P. Johnson, *Joining Together* (Englewood Cliffs, N.J.: Prentice-Hall, 1975), pp. 26-27; and Ron Nicholas et al., *Small Group Leaders' Handbook* (Downers Grove, Ill.: InterVarsity Press, 1982), pp. 64-67.

Chapter 6: The Life Cycle of a Group
[1]For helps on verbal communication see Nicholas, *Small Group Leaders' Handbook,* pp. 76-84.
[2]See Andrew Le Peau, *Paths of Leadership* (Downers Grove, Ill.: InterVarsity Press, 1983) for ways to encourage members to use their gifts in leading.

Chapter 7: How to Begin Small Groups and Make Them Multiply
[1]Clear help on how to lead an inductive Bible study can be found in Nicholas, *Small Group Leaders' Handbook,* chapter 10. See also pp. 86-89 in chapter 8 of the present book, "Preparing and Leading a Bible Study" in chapter 13, and the Nurture Resources in chapter 14.

Chapter 12: A Strategy for Small Groups in Your Church
[1]To explore this further see Donald McGavran, *Understanding Church Growth,* rev. ed. (Grand Rapids, Mich.: Eerdmans, 1980).
[2]Howard A. Snyder, *The Problem of Wineskins* (Downers Grove, Ill.: InterVarsity Press, 1975), p. 147.
[3]P. O. Box 3800, San Bernardino, CA 92413.

Chapter 13: Leadership Resources
[1]Allan Hart Johsmann, ed., *A Church Council Guidebook* (Philadelphia: Parish Life Press, 1982), pp. 19-20.
[2]Ibid., pp. 18-19.
[3]Ibid.

Select Bibliography

Leadership
Basic books for small group leaders

Griffin, Em. *Getting Together*. IVP, 1982.* Discusses task groups, relationship groups and influence groups, pointing out what makes for a good group in each. Topics covered: conflict, deviance, persuasion, expectations, leadership, having a good discussion.

Leadership. A publication of Christianity Today, Inc., 465 Gundersen Drive, Carol Stream, IL 60187. A practical journal for church leaders.

Le Peau, Andrew. *Paths of Leadership*. IVP, 1983. Good leadership is a group effort. Le Peau defines leadership in terms of serving, following, facilitating, teaching, modeling and envisioning.

Small Group Leaders' Handbook. IVP, 1982. A manual for IVCF student leaders but adaptable as a practical small group leaders' manual for the church as well.

Books to aid your vision for small groups

Coleman, Robert. *Master Plan of Evangelism*. Old Tappan, N.J.: Fleming H. Revell, 1978. A discussion of Jesus' three-year strategy to reach the ends of the earth. He began with a small group! Coleman focuses on Jesus' relationship with his disciples as a pattern for our own ministry.

Snyder, Howard. *Community of the King*. IVP, 1977. Examines the relationship between building community and expanding the kingdom, urging that gifts more than offices guide the operation of the church.

———. *Liberating the Church*. IVP, 1983. The church needs to be liberated for kingdom purposes. Snyder sees the church in the framework of the whole kingdom and economy of God.

———. *The Problem of Wineskins*. IVP, 1975. Discusses what kinds of church structures (wineskins) are most compatible with the gospel (wine) in our modern society, with the goal to foster church renewal. Shows how God's strategy has included small groups through the centuries.

---

*Books marked IVP are from InterVarsity Press, Downers Grove, Illinois 60515.

Practical helps for small group leaders

Augsburger, David. *Caring Enough to Confront.* Glendale, Calif.: Gospel Light, 1973. Encourages true communication and developing accountability in relationships.

Borman, Earnest C., and Borman, Nancy. *Effective Small Group Communication.* Minneapolis, Minn.: Burgess, 1980. A theory-plus-methods handbook for employing a small group approach to learning.

Leadership 100. A publication of Christianity Today, Inc., 465 Gundersen Drive, Carol Stream, IL 60187. A magazine where congregations pass on good ideas they have used in their church.

Nyquist, James, and Kuhatschek, Jack. *Leading Bible Discussions,* rev. ed. IVP, 1985. *The* book for all Bible study leaders. It gives practical field-tested suggestions for leaders in preparing, leading and evaluating Bible studies.

Williamson, David. *Group Power.* Englewood Cliffs, N.J.: Prentice-Hall, 1982. A practical book on the power of group life, the problems faced in groups, and ideas for handling these problems.

Nurture

Alexander, John W. *Scripture Memory 101.* IVP, 1975. A basic course in memorization. Includes reprints of 24 verses as a starter.

Colquhoun, Frank. *Hymns That Live.* IVP, 1980. Discusses the background, structure, language, content and message of forty traditional hymns.

Kunz, Marilyn. *Patterns for Living with God.* IVP, 1961. Illustrates God's presence and actions with twelve Old Testament characters, such as Caleb, Ruth and Daniel, whose lives have applications for today. 12-19 studies.

Kunz, Marilyn, and Schell, Catherine. Neighborhood Bible Study Guides. Wheaton, Ill.: Tyndale. These are excellent inductive study guides for small groups. They include studies to books in the Bible and several character studies.

Offner, Hazel. *The Fruit of the Spirit.* IVP, 1977. Passages from the Old and New Testaments which highlight the fruit of the Spirit summarized by Paul in Galatians 5:22-23. For individuals or groups. 9 studies.

Rough Edges of the Christian Life. IVP, 1972. Bible studies (for individuals or groups) on personal problems such as identity, lack of confidence, disobedience and depression. 8 studies.

Topical Memory System. Colorado Springs, Colo.: NavPress, 1969. Designed to help you memorize Scripture verses easily, apply them to your life and review them.

Wald, Oletta. *The Joy of Discovery.* Minneapolis, Minn.: Augsburg, 1975. A practical workbook for learning and practicing inductive Bible study. Shows you how to discover truths in the Bible and apply them to your life.

White, John. *The Fight.* IVP, 1976. Covers basic areas of the Christian life—prayer, Bible study, evangelism, faith, fellowship, work and guidance.

Worship

Colquhoun, Frank. *Hymns That Live.* IVP, 1980. Forty selected hymns come alive as the author sketches their background, examines their structure and language, and interprets their content and message.

Hallesby, O. *Prayer.* Minneapolis, Minn.: Augsburg, 1975. A classic that will change your perspective on prayer and on life. Chapters that might lead you to worship are "Difficulties in Prayer," "Wrestling in Prayer," "Forms of Prayer" and "The Spirit of Prayer."

Packer, James I. *Knowing God.* IVP, 1973. What were we made for? To know God. What aim should we set in life? To know God. What is the best thing in life? Knowledge of God. What in man gives God most pleasure? Knowledge of himself. Knowledge of God naturally leads to worship. Focus on the section "Behold Your God."

Rinker, R. *Prayer: Conversing with God.* Grand Rapids, Mich.: Zondervan, 1959. Helps reader learn to hold a two-way conversation with God. Several helps for personal and group prayer.

Tozer, A. W. *The Knowledge of the Holy.* New York: Harper & Row, 1978. "Written for plain persons whose hearts stir them up to seek after God Himself." Each chapter begins with a prayer and ends with a verse. The chapters are designed to help us appreciate God, especially his majesty and holiness.

White, John. *Daring to Draw Near.* IVP, 1977. Examines ten prayers from the Bible and helps us learn about prayer, God and those praying.

Community

Bonhoeffer, Dietrich. *Life Together.* New York: Harper & Row, 1976. A book for those who are hungry for true Christian fellowship. It is a window into what it means to be part of a Christian community: loving others, meeting God together, working together, eating together, ministering to one another, confessing to one another and having communion together.

Coleman, Lyman. *Encyclopedia of Serendipity.* Littleton, Colo.: Serendipity House, 1980. Suggestions for games, discussion topics and exercises your group can go through that will help you get to know one another better.

Fluegelmann, B. *New Games.* New York: Doubleday, 1976. A compilation of noncompetitive games from all over the world. They are marvelous at creating a structure around which your group can find out more about one another in a nonthreatening way.

Simon, Sidney. *Values Clarification.* New York: Hart, 1972. Several exercises which a group could use to help members understand themselves and share themselves better with others.

Mission

Bryant, David. *In the Gap.* 1979. Reprint ed.; Ventura, Calif.: Regal Books, 1984.

This handbook describes what a world Christian is, how he thinks and how he chooses and acts for Christ's global cause. Provides a framework for thinking "world Christian" and a wealth of ideas and resources for developing a world-Christian lifestyle. A small group study guide is enclosed, providing a nine-week study/discussion of the book and its implications.

Ford, Leighton. *Good News Is for Sharing.* Elgin, Ill.: David C. Cook, 1977. Sharing good news is a lifestyle patterned after God. It is a life of making friends for God as God has made us his friends through his Son.

Hopler, Thom. *A World of Difference: Following Christ beyond Your Cultural Walls.* IVP, 1981. A cultural survey of the Bible, applying this teaching to the modern world, highlighting the profound impact of urbanization on people both in and out of the city. A group study guide is also available with twelve discussions, suggested activities and exercises.

Johnstone, P. J. *Operation World: A Handbook for World Intercession.* Bromley, Kent, England: STL Publications, revised annually. A catalog of facts about every country in the world with prayer requests for each. (Also available from I-V Missions, Madison, WI 53703.)

Little, Paul. *How to Give Away Your Faith.* IVP, 1966. A biblical, relevant and practical look at evangelism. It answers questions like, What is a Christian? How do you witness? How do you hurdle social barriers? What is the message? Why believe? What is the role of faith in evangelism? Is Christianity relevant? What is worldliness?

————. *Know Why You Believe.* Rev. ed. IVP, 1968. Shows how Christianity consistently addresses itself to major problems: Is there a God? Do science and Scripture conflict? Why does God allow suffering and evil? Is Christianity relevant?

Lum, Ada. *How to Lead an Evangelistic Bible Study.* IVP, 1971. Ada Lum tells how Christians can initiate and lead an evangelistic Bible study with their non-Christian friends.

Metzger, Will. *Tell the Truth.* 2d ed. IVP, 1984. The author helps us tell the truth—the whole truth—with a comprehensive presentation of what it means for whole people to offer the whole gospel to the whole of a person's life. A book for those wanting to grow in God-centered witnessing. Includes a training manual with worksheets.

Pippert, Rebecca. *Out of the Saltshaker.* IVP, 1979. A basic guide to evangelism as a natural way of life, emphasizing the pattern set by Jesus. It will help you relax and be honest about yourself and your life in Christ. It gives practical help in shaping a conversational style, understanding reasons for your faith and seeing the role of the Christian community in witness.

Prayer Cards (for individual countries). Send the Light, Inc., P.O. Box 148, Midland Park, NJ 07432.

World map or atlas.

Index of Resources